How to Commit Monogamy

How to Commit Monogamy

A Lighthearted Look at Long-Term Love

Elaine Viets

Andrews McMeel
Publishing

Kansas City

Library of Congress Cataloging-in-Publication Data

Viets, Elaine, 1950–
   How to commit monogamy : a lighthearted look at long-term love /
Elaine Viets.
      p. cm.
   ISBN 0-8362-2723-9 (hd)
   1. Marriage—United States. 2. Married people—United States.
I. Title.
HQ536.V54   1997
306.81—dc21   96–52625
                                                                  CIP

Design and composition by Top Dog Design

To Don

who can wiggle both ears at once

Acknowledgments

Many thanks to my agent, the hardworking David Hendin.

Special thanks to my editor Jean Lowe at Andrews and McMeel for her sensitive editing job. Thanks also to editorial assistant Richard Hill, who can track down anything.

I also want to thank Edward O. Laumann, George Herbert Mead Distinguished Professor of Sociology and Chairman of the Department of Sociology at the University of Chicago, for his valuable interview concerning the National Health and Social Life Survey.

Thanks to Anne Watts for her skilled research and to the staff of the St. Louis Public Library for answering all those difficult questions.

Many other people helped make this book possible. They include: John Bell and Orene Contini, Charles Brennan of KMOX Radio, Susan Burney, Richard Buthod of The BookSource, Elea Carey, Susan Carlson, John Carney at KTRS Radio, David Craig and Debbie Conner at WIL Radio, Lorraine Dieckmeyer, Laurie Dohse, Kelli Eggers at KPLR-TV, Tom Finan, Nancy and Dick Friedman, Jinny Gender, Ruth Gerchen, Ed Goodman and Mary Phelan at KEZK Radio, Karen Grace, Sarah Hendin, Debbie Henson, Dan Hill of Botanicals on the Park, Betty Hoeffner, Kevin Horrigan of KTRS Radio, Janice Bequette Jones, Rosemary Kochner, Marilyn Koehr, Cindy Lane, Charlene LaRosa, Robert Levine, the Rev. Scott Lohse, Betty and Paul Mattli, Mike McCarthy and Ellyn McManus, Guy Phillips and Michelle Dibble of KYKY Radio, Dick Richmond, Maria Sacco, Sue Savage, Jay and Jeanne Schober, Craig Schwab of KFNS Radio, Janet Smith, Susan Spanel of the *St. Louis Times,* Judy Taylor, Jean Toenjes, Donna O'Toole, Uncle Bill's Pancake House, Laurie Waters of KMOV-TV, Walter Veazey, Allan Zerman. And, finally, thanks to those sources who must remain anonymous.

Contents

FOREWORD
I Committed Monogamy

Don and I made a shocking discovery on our anniversary.

"How long have we been married?" Don asked.

"Twenty-five years," I said.

The words sounded like a prison sentence. Don and I looked at each other in horror. "Only old people are married that long," Don said.

"Worse. Only middle-aged people are married that long," I said.

Would he have to start wearing plaid shorts, black socks, and sandals? Would I wear curlers to bed? Would we snore little duets together?

Previous generations bragged about the married years they'd racked up, like cons with long-term prison sentences. But we baby boomers believe in quality time. Two to five years sounds nicely newlywed. Seven to ten can be interesting and itchy. Even fifteen sounds fun.

But twenty-five years with the same person? You must be brain dead. We look at these couples and wonder, "What's wrong?"

Weren't you in therapy?

Don't you have the job skills to break free?

Don't you have any pride? If you had any gumption you'd get divorced at least once. How can you be such a stick-in-the-mud?

Didn't you have any self-awareness in the seventies? Couldn't you find a good lawyer in the eighties?

Married people have nothing to talk about. We can't swap stories about our exes. We have no custody battles. We don't have a year when we lived with someone unsuitable. We can't tell you about the race-car driver, the stripper, or the bum who used to borrow money from us. We were married then.

We didn't even live together for a respectable five or ten years first. We rushed down the aisle like it was 1950.

We don't have an interesting postmarital arrangement. We're not staying together until the children get through college. We're not hanging on because of the community property laws. We don't have an understanding that we live together but go our separate ways.

We're married. It's so unoriginal.

People married that long can't have a romance. Not with each other, anyway. When they get that hot, fluttery feeling, they go to the doctor for a checkup.

Don and I have tried so hard to be young. We've dieted, worked out, and gotten our gossip from *Vanity Fair*. And now, through no fault of our own, we make each other look old.

Lately, we've tried cheating. Because Don and I have different last names, we try to give the impression we're living together. Sometimes when we're traveling, Don will register ahead at the motel as single and then sneak me in. It sets the right tone. Saves money, too. We don't feel quite so out of it when the hotel clerk tactfully asks, "Do you want one room key or two?"

My favorite scene happened in the bar of a resort hotel.

Don wanted to sign the bar tab. "The room's not in my name," he told the bartender.

"That's okay," said the bartender, smiling. "You're a known companion."

The guy on the next bar stool snickered. I felt so proud. I didn't correct the bartender. I didn't want him to think we were married.

I don't know how we went wrong. Our marriage started with such a promising scandal. Don was my college English teacher. He was thirty-one. I was ten years younger. The entire campus was shocked by our romance. This was not what the university meant by student affairs.

My parents opposed our marriage right up to the hour before the wedding. "You can call it off, and we'll just have a big party," Mom said. I ignored her and put on my wedding dress.

Don's mother was shocked, too. She hated that I looked so young. She refused to give her hometown paper, the Marshalltown, Iowa, *Times-Republican*, my engagement picture. "People will think Don married you for only one thing," she told me.

She was right.

I didn't expect it to be so long or so hard. But monogamy is like that. You try it for a year. Then another. And another. Before you know it, you're labeled a practicing monogamist. No matter how scandalous your past, most people believe monogamy is as exciting as two matched socks.

No one sees sex with a married man (when he's *your* married man) as any fun. You're supposed to complain about how he sits around the house like a potted plant. That's proper monogamous behavior.

But I don't think it is. I'm getting hints that in secret, behind closed doors, some people find monogamy exciting and satisfying. They're embarrassed by this discovery. Only a few are willing to talk about it.

But I've found some of them. I can tell you about the fifty-year-old woman whose husband bought her a Harley for their twenty-fifth wedding anniversary. She bought herself the studded black-leather bustier to wear while she rides it. Of course, she doesn't wear leather or ride her Harley to play bridge at the country club.

And the man who agreed to quit drinking if his wife would go to a nudist camp. Can you imagine the average married man asking such a thing? Elmer thought he could safely swill forever. He knew his wife would never walk around naked in front of strangers. But her answer knocked Elmer right off his bar stool. Monogamy is full of surprises.

Here's another surprise: Americans are good at monogamy. We're learning how to handle it with humor and style. We're also learning to work out the rules for this generation's two-career marriages. We're learning how to handle each other's failures, successes, and money. We work out how often to go to office parties and dinners at relatives. We make lasting promises and short-term bargains.

We try to understand that monogamy is nothing to be ashamed of.

After all, few Americans escape it, at least for a little while. By age thirty, about 90 percent of us have been married.

This book will help you survive the embarrassment of long-term monogamy. You can live with it. You can even learn to enjoy it.

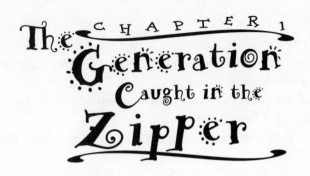

CHAPTER 1
The Generation Caught in the Zipper

Most Americans are monogamous.

Forget what you see on *The Oprah Winfrey Show*, read in Ann Landers, and watch in the movies. The sex statistics say we're oozing virtue.

More than 80 percent of adults had one sex partner—or none—in the past year, according to a major sex survey.

Keep in mind that the sociologist's definition of monogamy is different from the way your mother, your teacher, and your preacher explained it. It's also not quite what you promised at the altar. Sex science says monogamy is one partner for one year—sort of like sobriety except you take it a year at a time.

This version of monogamy is much easier than that ominous marriage vow where you promise "till death do us part." That can have you looking around for a .38-caliber divorce fairly fast.

Faithfulness is one record we should be proud of: We Americans stick to our partners, day in and day out, 365 days a year.

Instead, we're deeply ashamed.

For instance, when the University of Chicago did its

famous 1994 survey on American sexual habits, it said more than 80 percent of us were monogamous. We behaved ourselves for a whole year.

How did the press play this national virtue?

They turned it into a fault.

SURVEY FINDS MOST ADULTS SEXUALLY STAID, said the *Washington Post*.

In the staid Midwest, the *St. Louis Post-Dispatch* said: 'HEAVY SEX?' SURVEY FINDS LITTLE OF IT—FAITHFULNESS THE RULE; OBSESSION THE EXCEPTION.

Why make this news into a national negative?

Because monogamy has such a bad name. Look at some of the people who are trying to get you to commit monogamy.

The first is Phyllis Schlafly, the woman who works to keep women in the home. Her Eagle Forum prescribes monogamy like medicine. The Forum uses it as a cure for genital herpes. "There is only one way to be sure you never get herpes: avoid sexual relations," the Forum's pamphlet says. "Remain a virgin until you marry, marry a virgin, and remain faithful to each other."

You can't argue with advice like that. Of course, those of us who are not virgins are out of luck.

Then there's the Pope, a man who never tried monogamy but helped tighten the screws so American Catholics have a harder time getting out of it. Divorce is out, the Vatican declared in a letter to the world's bishops. If you remarry and don't get a church annulment, you should not receive communion unless you repent and abstain from sex with your new partner.

At least you won't get herpes.

Even if you're still married to your first partner, you're not supposed to have fun. You're supposed to have children. Children, said the Pope, "constitute the fruit of love of one man and of one woman."

He is absolutely right. But I do think if the Pope got slapped upside the head by a drunken spouse or cleaned grape jelly fingerprints off the Vatican woodwork, he'd have a broader view of monogamy.

But why pick on the Pope? Church leaders such as Jimmy Swaggart, Jerry "Moral Majority" Falwell, and Jim Bakker have all clutched monogamy to their bosoms. Then, when they have ungodly adventures, it only confirms everyone's opinion: Monogamy is next to impossible.

Jimmy Swaggart was defrocked after frolicking twice with hookers. The first time, he kept on preaching without credentials and promised never to stray again.

The second time, Jimmy swerved from the path of righteousness (and the road) in a Jaguar. He got caught with a prostitute and a car full of girlie magazines. When his long-suffering flock complained, he said God told them to mind their own business.

We got our own message, and it didn't come from God: Monogamy was for hypocrites.

It doesn't help when government leaders keep coming out foursquare for monogamy. One of the most persistent is Senator Jesse Helms, the man who tried to show "the Ah-mur-ican pee-pull" Robert Mapplethorpe's bullwhip pictures on C-SPAN. Jesse is constantly trying to divert money to a right-wing program pushing monogamy for teenagers. Listen to Jesse talk about monogamy in the *Congressional Record*:

> The Title XX Program's message . . . is that it is healthier — physically, psychologically, and from an economic standpoint—to forego sexual relations until marriage. And, Mr. President, that message is anathema to the crowd, for example,

that went out to my house in Arlington, Virginia,
last week and stretched a big canvas condom over
the top of it. They do not like me and I do not
like them.

Then there's George Bush, the president who pushed
family values. Ugh. Just the kind of man to give monogamy
a bad name. In her autobiography, Barbara Bush tells of the
time George was out of town and woke her up with a 5:30
A.M. phone call to ask: "How's the big guy?"

He was asking about his dog.

Monogamy is so straight. So unsatisfying. So unsophisti-
cated. Glamorous Jack Kennedy was not monogamous.
Wimpy loser George Bush is. George (isn't that a monogamous name?) is typical of the kind of people who are willing to admit they are monogamous.

It doesn't matter that George Bush is worth millions,
used to be president of the United States, and probably
doesn't mow his own lawn (or anyone else's). His unexciting
brand of monogamy is the only kind we knew about when
I was a kid. We thought marriage had to be like that.

I grew up in the suburbs in the sixties, and monogamy
was rampant. Everyone was married. Everyone had kids.
Everything was alike. All the houses were split-levels or
ranch houses with aluminum siding. All the dads went to
work. All the moms stayed home and kept house. There was
no such thing as a gay couple or a single mother. Black people and old people lived in the city. Jewish people lived in
New York.

The most exotic person I saw was a Methodist. One of
our neighbors had a "mixed marriage." I was fascinated by
my first up-close view. The Methodist mom looked just like
our moms, but I knew from religion class that she had a

three-in-one chance of being damned in hell. Catholics, thanks to confession, didn't have to be so careful.

The only divorced person I knew was my Aunt Rickie, and she lived in the city. My family sent me out of the room when they talked about Aunt Rickie. The few times I was allowed to see her, I thought she was a fascinating creature. She wore an ankle bracelet, which was wicked. She had red lipstick and bright yellow hair the color of new brass. Even I knew it was dyed.

Aunt Rickie owned a city saloon with a jukebox, two pool tables, and signs on the bathroom doors that said POINTERS and SETTERS. She let me guzzle orange soda until my belly swelled like a balloon. Generosity was her main fault.

She was not monogamous. I knew she had a lot of "boy-friends" (that's what she called them), because I saw them at the bar. Some of them had jobs and all their teeth. But I had no idea what she did with them. Aunt Rickie never talked about sex around me. If I asked any questions she clammed up tighter than her closed cash register.

There was no one like Aunt Rickie in my suburb of Florissant, Missouri. Women there would not be caught dead in ankle bracelets. They always wore "nice" dresses and heels to church, and they went to church even more than they went shopping. They didn't dye their hair interesting colors like Aunt Rickie, although they did cover their gray with a light rinse. My mother explained that her hair went gray overnight at age thirty-five, from shock, when she heard of her grandfather's death. I believed her until I turned thirty-five, woke up in the morning, and saw I had more gray hair than I could ever pull out.

I had to admit, it was a shock. I went to the beauty shop and turned brunette overnight.

The women in my suburb didn't look as sexy as Aunt Rickie, but I figured there had to be a lot of sex going on because they had so many kids. My family was small, with only four children. Families with six, eight, or even twelve kids were common.

If children were the fruits of monogamy, they were pretty rotten—at least in my view. I spent every evening and most weekends baby-sitting the little fruits. This was before Nintendo, and their favorite pastimes seemed to be punching and kicking each other. A few nights with them, and I decided abortion should be retroactive. I was getting rich baby-sitting. In just one summer, I'd racked up $83.50, working for fifty cents an hour, but at what price?

I figured I must be missing something with this monogamy business. I needed to know more. My mother's friends used to sit around her kitchen table, drinking coffee and gossiping. The talk got interesting if the kids weren't around. When the women gathered to sink reputations with Sanka, I ostentatiously announced I was going up to my room to study. If I closed my door and sat by the furnace grate next to my dresser, I could hear everything they said. I had only a sketchy knowledge of sex, based on a Girl Scout lecture and some stuff I overheard in the girls' bathroom at school. So these were educational sessions.

I learned that Shelley's premature baby weighed nine pounds, six ounces.

I heard that Mrs. Meyer met the mailman at the front door in her bathing suit—in the middle of winter.

And Mrs. O'Hara, the transplanted Southern belle, left her vacuum cleaner out in the middle of the living room for her husband to carry to the upstairs closet, for God's sake, like she was some kinda cripple. Funny, the women said, she could haul in those dress boxes without any help.

But the best times were when the women would lower their voices and talk about sex with their husbands. Then I'd have to get flat on the floor and press my ear against the metal grate to hear everything. One day, Mrs. Mettermann confessed that she had figured out a way to watch Johnny Carson while she and her husband . . . you know . . . did it . . . during Johnny's monologue. She didn't miss a joke, and Jim never guessed a thing.

Between their shrieks and giggles, I couldn't figure out exactly how she managed it. But it had something to do with putting the TV on the chest of drawers and moving her left foot forward.

When the giggles died down, another woman, Mrs. Figby, said she also found Johnny Carson useful. She talked her husband into staying up for the monologue every night. Johnny left him weak with laughter. He could barely make it up the stairs, and when he hit the bed he went straight to sleep, no fooling around.

After all, he had to get up at six A.M.

This set off another round of giggles and snickers. It also left me puzzled. I was sure both these women liked sex. After all, Mrs. Mettermann had five kids, and Mrs. Figby had four. Mrs. Mettermann was kind of old and scrawny, but her husband was well preserved for a man going on thirty-five.

Did this mean Johnny Carson was better than married sex?

But sex was such a powerful temptation, the Catholic Church said it was a mortal sin unless you were married.

Even then it was still a mortal sin unless you did it with the person you were married to. And then it could still be a mortal sin unless you did it the right way. You could burn in hell for sex. So far as I could figure out, watching Johnny Carson wasn't a sin at all. Even nuns stayed up for his monologue.

I listened carefully to Johnny Carson, trying to figure out his mysterious power. Just thinking about what was going on in my neighborhood during his monologue made his jokes spicier. For weeks the women giggled over Johnny and Mrs. Mettermann. All they had to do was say his name and someone would break into snickers.

Then one morning Mrs. Mettermann came over for coffee. She sat down and burst out crying. She was pregnant— again—baby number six.

And she blamed Johnny Carson.

Through her tears and their sympathetic noises, all I could hear was that she got to laughing during one of Johnny's monologues, and someone—or something—slipped. "And my youngest goes into the first grade in September," she wailed.

I was old enough to know what that meant. A woman who had all her kids in school full-time was free. She could have the day to herself. She could shop, do serious house cleaning, have a quiet cup of coffee by herself. She could even act like a lady and do a little genteel volunteer work.

Now Mrs. Mettermann was trapped in years of baby business: washing diapers, sterilizing bottles, lugging diaper bags, not to mention the baby, everywhere she went. She had to go through late-night feedings, teething, potty training, and other traumas all over again. The women sat together in stricken silence.

One thing was for sure, if it was a boy, Mrs. Mettermann wasn't going to call him Johnny.

That night, when my parents turned on Johnny Carson, my father howled at the monologue. But my mother didn't laugh very loud. I listened to a few jokes but went to bed before the monologue was over.

What Johnny Carson did to Mrs. Mettermann wasn't funny.

No wonder my generation just said no. There are no good

monogamous role models. The monogamy I grew up with seemed so awful, it gave me nightmares. When I was in high school, I began to have the same dream over and over. In the dream, I was getting married. I wore a long white dress and veil. I walked down the aisle with my husband-to-be, a faceless figure who looked a lot like the guy on my cousin's wedding cake. When we got to the altar, we climbed into a coffin. The lid was shut. The coffin was delivered to the split-level across the street from my house.

Then I woke up screaming.

Marriage, suburban style, was not for me. It looked as if I had no choice but to wear an ankle bracelet and be a bad girl. Maybe I could have my own city saloon, like Aunt Rickie. I knew unless I had time for a deathbed confession, I'd have to spend eternity in hell, but what the heck. It sounded more interesting than life in the suburbs. And I was sure it wouldn't last as long.

But I had a problem. I liked only one boy at a time. Right then it was Joe, who had green eyes and the nicest curl on his forehead. When he boldly kissed me in his pink-and-white 1964 Rambler right in the driveway of my house, my ears popped and I saw bright lights.

The bright lights were because my mother had flicked on the porch light. She didn't want the Martins, our next-door neighbors, to get the wrong idea about me. But I wondered what was wrong with these suburban women? Why didn't they like kissing? I decided it must be monogamy. It ruined your sex life.

The boomers are the first generation to publicly reject monogamy. Even if we are monogamous, we won't admit it.

After all, we have our pride. We came of age in the swinging sixties. We still see ourselves as bold bed hoppers. "Sex, drugs, and rock and roll" was our generation's motto.

Better to let our kids think we ran wild at Woodstock than to let them know we never strayed from the path of virtue. Well, hardly ever. Except for those six months after our divorce when we screwed everybody including the dishwasher repairman. And statistically, that doesn't count.

What we really don't like to admit, especially to ourselves, is that the generation raised on Ozzie and Harriet and June and Ward Cleaver really does want to love one person.

And we have.

A surprising number of boomers have been married twenty years or more. Sometimes we logged that time with one person. Sometimes we had two or three spouses. But we were still faithful in our fashion.

We are still working out some model of marriage. We knew we didn't want our parents' marriages. The late Erma Bombeck was our mother's role model. Erma painted herself as a smart frump, unhappy with her suburban life, but unable to break out of it.

Poor Erma. We didn't want that. We wanted to go to work. We saw a job as a cure-all, god help us. When we married, we put in strict safeguards to stay sexy. We knew what our mother's generation did wrong. If we didn't sleep in curlers or wear flannel pajamas with feet, our marriage would stay romantic forever. If we didn't get fat, he would stay in love with us, wouldn't he? We might be starved for food, but we'd never be starved for love. Our love life, at least, would stay hot and juicy.

The women of my mother's generation were fine people, but please, god, don't let us sit in the kitchen and cackle about our husbands the love duds. Let Mom and her friends read *The Joy of Cooking*. We read *The Joy of Sex*.

We also read in Gay Talese's *Thy Neighbor's Wife* that Alex Comfort, the man who cooked up that sex book, joined in the orgies at Sandstone Retreat, the fifteen-acre California estate for sexually free couples. Watergate figure Daniel Ellsberg also frolicked there.

Wow. Those were role models. I was proud of them, even though I'd never been to an orgy and probably never would be. I was married, remember? Besides, I wasn't sure what to do afterward. Do you shake hands with these former strangers? Do you write thank-you notes for the lovely time?

At least I had the satisfaction of knowing the nice suburban mothers I grew up with wouldn't approve of those books. That was enough. My goal was not to grow up to be Erma Bombeck and her friends. There's such a thing as too good a woman.

But we couldn't be too bad, either. Most of us weren't quite Erica Jong. Sure, I admire the woman. Maybe Erica could do it "zipless" on an airplane. But I couldn't even get to the john without standing in line at thirty thousand feet. And I wouldn't know what to do when it was over. You can't even light up a cigarette in airplane restrooms anymore.

We are somewhere between zipped-up Erma and zipless Erica, trying to work out our version of monogamy.

We're the generation caught in the zipper.

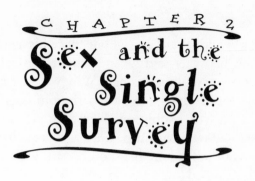

CHAPTER 2

Sex and the Single Survey

The summer I was seventeen, our subdivision simmered with seduction and betrayal. An August of adultery was ushered in by midnight screams. The whole family was awakened by pounding on our front door. It was Katy, who lived in the split-level with the black shutters. She howled to my mother and the summer moon, "Send out your husband! Send out your husband! You never share him with me. You never share."

Katy drank a little. She was not an alcoholic because there were no alcoholics in nice neighborhoods. But sometimes Katy got carried away with the whiskey sours. Mom and Dad threw on some clothes and helped the weeping Katy home while the neighbors peered out their windows or stood on their carports in pajamas and robes.

Nobody said another word about this episode to Katy—but they sure talked behind her back.

After that, it was like someone lifted off all the roofs in our subdivision, so I could see the lives inside. Every bedroom, bush, and station wagon backseat seemed to have an adulterous couple.

A teenage boy in our subdivision bragged to me that he

was having sex with Patsy, a neighbor twice his age. The kid was cute, but his sister said he spent hours in front of the bathroom mirror combing his hair. Why would Patsy risk a hardworking husband for a teenage bathroom hogger?

Patsy was no Mrs. Robinson. Her Bermuda shorts and tops were stained with baby urp. Kids' toys crunched underfoot when you walked in her house. She always looked ready to fall into bed—for a good twenty hours' sleep.

Next, the grade school teacher was seen necking on a back road with her friend's husband. I never figured out how they did it in a Volkswagen.

And finally, one of the men who passed the collection basket at church had too much beer and told me the lady who ironed the altar cloths propositioned him.

I was shocked. The church lady wore granny underwear. I'd seen those flabby white cotton panties flapping on her clothesline. Women with ugly underwear did not hit on other people's husbands.

The whole subdivision was in the throes of illicit passion, and I waited for the consequences. Something tragic had to happen. That summer, I'd read two Russian novels, a forbidden copy of *Lady Chatterley's Lover,* and every mystery in the bookmobile. I knew someone would commit suicide, be killed by a jealous spouse, or be driven mad by grief and shame.

Nothing happened. The wandering women worried whether they should serve creamed corn or canned green beans with the sirloin tip roast they made for their cuckolded husbands. They picked up their kids at the pool and shopped for school supplies at Kmart.

The straying husbands puttered around the yard and barbecued on Saturday. The studly kid ducked his mother when she wanted him to take out the trash.

Even adultery was boring in Florissant.

But I wasn't surprised when I saw all those polls and sci-entific surveys showing married people cheated like crazy. Here's a small sampling:

Seventy percent of married men play around, says *Playboy*.

Seventy percent of women are unfaithful after five years or more of marriage, says *The Hite Report, Women and Love: A Cultural Revolution in Progress.*

Fifty percent of married men cheat. Twenty-six percent of women are unfaithful, says Kinsey, the daddy of all sex researchers.

"Thirty-six percent of women and 48 percent of men have sex outside a relationship that is supposed to be mo-nogamous," says a *Mademoiselle* magazine survey.

Of course, the University of Chicago's National Health and Social Life survey says that more than 80 percent of Americans (and more than 94 percent of married Ameri-cans) were monogamous in the past year.

But what did they know? Look at all the adultery in my suburb.

I did notice that some of those bed-hopping statistics sounded a little confused. Are 70 percent of the Hite wives running around with 50 percent of the Kinsey husbands? If so, who's seeing the other 20 percent of the straying Hite wives?

Maybe these women hit on unmarried mailmen and meter readers—or slept around with *Playboy* husbands.

The results seemed confusing. In fact, I couldn't figure out how bad we were at monogamy. That's when I realized many surveys have a major problem: unfaithfulness.

The survey takers strayed from strict scientific methods.

Their exciting sex information, clad only in the barest facts, easily seduces the media. I'm sorry to say that my profession is easy—and I say this as a columnist who's fallen hard for several surveys with soft data. We lust after any sexy science story. If it's a slow news week, we will chase after another sleazy survey. We can't get enough of it, knocking off one piece after another.

Why do we fall for the first survey that comes around?

Because most editors and reporters can't tell when a survey is bad. We took journalism in college so we wouldn't have to slog through math or science. I barely limped out of Econ 51 with a C—and it was specially designed for mush-brained journalists.

We should beware of any survey conducted by a magazine polling its readers. Surveys of *Redbook, Playboy,* and *Mademoiselle* readers simply tell you what the magazine's readers are up to—and only a small sample of those. And that tells you very little about the rest of us. Does your husband read *Playboy?* Do you still read *Mademoiselle?* Do these magazines have anything to do with you?

A few years ago, *Mademoiselle* claimed to have the "ultimate sex survey." The results were shocking: 36 percent of the women in the survey had sex outside of a monogamous relationship. More than one-quarter couldn't remember the first and last names of all their sex partners.

At best, you could call this risky behavior in the nineties. At worst, it's pretty slutty. Who are these women and how do you keep them away from your husband?

Here's the catch. The average woman who answered the *Mademoiselle* sex survey was twenty-two years old and unmarried. Notice that word "unmarried." Those *Mademoiselle* statistics won't tell you a thing about monogamy in marriage.

Next, we should ask this: Was the survey promiscuous? Did it let anyone answer its questions? Or did it seek out a proper representative sampling?

I could find you enough examples to fill the rest of this book. But let's consider one: *The Hite Report, Women and Love: A Cultural Revolution in Progress.* Shere Hite hit hard at men and monogamy. She begins her book with, "Women are suffering a lot of pain in their love relationships with men."

So how did Hite measure the depth of female pain?

She mailed 100,000 questionnaires to clubs and organizations including "church groups in thirty-four states, women's voting and political groups in nine states, women's rights organizations in thirty-nine states, professional women's groups in twenty-two states, counseling and walk-in centers for women or families in forty-three states, and a wide range of other organizations, such as senior citizens' homes and disabled people's organizations, in various states."

This is a variety, all right, but it's a variety of joiners. What about women who hate to join anything? What about women who don't have time?

Here is something else to chew on: Wouldn't these organizations have a lot of zealots? The godly members of the East Jesus Ladies' Prayer Circle can be just as fanatic as the godless NOW members. Counseling and walk-in centers for women might have high numbers of the abused and unhappily married. *The Hite Report* doesn't seem to represent a true range of women.

Here's another question that should be asked about surveys like Hite's: Why did the entire population of Burbank, California, turn her down?

Hite says forty-five hundred women answered her questionnaire. But she sent out 100,000 questionnaires. That means 95,500 women declined. That's more than all the people in beautiful Burbank.

Why did so many women say no?

And what about the ones who said yes?

Hite has a trusting faith that the women answered honestly. But I think she underestimates her fellow men. What's keeping the teenage son of the Figby Township Republican Women's Club from glomming some questionnaires and filling them out for a joke?

Indeed, *Interview* magazine reveals that male treachery reached a new Hite. It says, "One of her ex-doormen has claimed he and his friends filled in several questionnaires with outrageous responses, only to find them published in one of her books."

I can't entirely blame the doorman. The questionnaire had an outrageous effect on me. Hite asks questions like these: "Have you ever masturbated with a partner? During intercourse? During general caresses? Was it hard to do the first time? How did you feel? What was his/her reaction? Do you have your legs together or apart for orgasm?"

Her questions come faster and faster, until you can't help yourself, you answer and a great wave of relief comes over you, and you can't remember if your legs are together or apart.

Reading Hite's breathless questions is like being pursued by the biggest gossip in the neighborhood. He happens to be a man, by the way. He's an old guy in baggy pants who owns an even baggier beagle. That dog must have the smallest bladder in the city. The neighbor walks the dog fifty times a day—past all the delivery vans, FedEx trucks, parked police cars, even lawn crews and painting parties. He checks out all your visitors, packages, and flower deliveries.

Under the guise of neighborly concern, he stops you on the sidewalk and peppers you with questions: "I saw you had the air-conditioning man again," he says. "That's twice this week now, isn't it? A little unusual for this time of year, yes? Was it the compressor? Is it the unit on the roof or under the deck?"

On and on, he probes and pumps, until you crack like a rotten porch timber. You denounce all repair persons, show him your bill, anything to shut him up. But you resent this neighbor's prying.

That's how the Hite questions affected me. They seemed designed to stir up subtle resentments. Consider the effects of the first few questions in a section called "Your Current Relationship":

"What is the most important part of this relationship, the reason you want it? Is it love, passion, sexual intimacy, economics, daily companionship, or the long-term value of a family relationship? Other?"

Yes, all of it. Although I must say, the long-term value of the family relationship is a real downer. Did I ever tell you about the time his aunt showed up, unannounced, and stayed for six weeks? She expected to be waited on hand and foot. Must run in that family. Of course, he never lets me forget about my relative, who accidentally packed the TV set when he left.

Oops, let me see, I'm off the track here . . . what is the next question?

"Are you happy with the relationship? Inspired? What do you like most and least about it? Can you imagine spending the rest of your life in it? Is your partner happy?"

Happy? Of course *he's* happy. I do 90 percent of the work. He thinks making the bed is doing the housework. He wouldn't know how to scrub a toilet if he had a Glock semiautomatic in his gut. As for cleaning the cat box, I guess he thinks I've trained the cat to scoop out after himself. Hah. Fat chance. The cat's a slob, too. But what can you expect?

It's a male cat. At least I had the animal neutered. That's one relationship where I got total satisfaction.

You can see why *The Hite Report* should be questioned. Can't you? How do you feel about that? When did you first begin to feel like that? Did you like it? Were your legs open or closed?

Why blame the women who survey? The men are just as bad—even the biggies like Kinsey. Kinsey also used some groups to answer his sex questions. Sometimes, he had a captive audience. Yep, about one-quarter of the men were "former or present prisoners; a high percentage were sex offenders . . ." says the scholarly *Society.* He interviewed "at least 200 male prostitutes."

And these people are being compared to your husband.

Did Kinsey really think the average family man would behave like male prostitutes, sex offenders, and convicts? No wonder his men had a 50 percent rate of infidelity. You're probably surprised the numbers are so low.

After hearing these stories, you must wonder: Are there any good surveys out there? Surveys you can trust? Surveys with decent data that won't lie to you? Of course. No matter how many bad surveys you've met, you mustn't let them poison your attitude toward all surveys. There are some fine surveys.

Let me introduce you to one of the better surveys, the National Health and Social Life Survey by researchers at the University of Chicago. This survey took time to know people. No anonymous mail quickies. It used face-to-face interviews that lasted ninety minutes, so nobody's doorman could have fun with these questions. Yet it also had a way to answer embarrassing questions privately. And no survey takers dropped by the prison. This survey had a carefully chosen representative sample of 3,432 people.

The results make you proud to be monogamous. Here's what the University of Chicago researchers found, as reported in their book *Sex in America*:

- **Most married people are faithful.** "Ninety-four percent had one partner in the past year. Couples who were living together were almost as faithful."
- **Married people have more sex than the so-called swinging singles.** "About 40 percent have sex with their partner two or more times a week." Less than 25 percent of singles got that much.
- **Married people have more satisfying sex.** "Among married women, 75 percent reported always or usually having an orgasm during sex, compared with 62 percent of single women."
- **Married people are more sexually satisfied.** "The people who reported being the most physically pleased and emotionally satisfied were the married couples." Cohabiting couples did well, too.
- **Married people were more emotionally satisfied.** "The lowest rates of satisfaction were among men and women who were neither married nor living with someone—the very group thought to be having the hottest sex."
- **Cheating on your partner does not double your fun.** "People who have extramarital partners or those who are unmarried and who have several partners in a year actually end up having partnered sex less often than people who have only one partner. The sole exceptions were the 5 percent of men who had five or more partners in a year; they had sex slightly more often than people with a single partner."
- **Adults do not have more fun in adultery.** "Our data also show that married or cohabiting people who have a second partner, like the husband with a lover he sees regularly

or the girlfriend who is still seeing her old lover on the side, were less happy with their sex lives. And these people seemed to get more pleasure from sex with their primary partner, their spouse or person they were living with, than they did with their secondary partners."

The survey results were also proeducation. They found that people who went to college were more likely to have oral sex. And have more sex partners. And do more interesting things with them.

Ever since D. H. Lawrence, we've been led to believe that poorly educated men are better lovers than effete university grads. This survey says Mellors the Gamekeeper would be conventional and conservative in bed. If you want the exotic moves, marry someone who's had some college.

This information could give high school teachers new ammunition to help students go on to higher education. I can hear Miss Cranblow lecturing now: "If you drop out of high school, James, you may never get a blow job. Don't you want to know what that's like? Then stay in school and study hard."

Mothers can tell their daughters: "Have an affair with that carny barker if you want, Millicent. But once you get past his fascinating LOVE-HATE tattoo, the man will be abysmally uninspired. And he'll never go down on you. That nice college boy will be better in bed. Besides, his tattoo washes off. Someday, that will be important."

Despite those findings about education, the survey showed that married people have one thing in common, no matter what their race, religion, age, or income:

Married people are nearly all alike—they are faithful to their partners as long as the marriage is intact, says *Sex in America*. They usually stray only when the marriage is breaking up. They may have several sex partners when they are divorced and looking for a new mate. But when they are married, most are faithful.

One more thing. If you watch the movies and soaps, you assume that the average single American has sex in the morning, at night, and between meals. All you and your husband can manage is sex two or three times a week. That must be because you're married.

Wrong, Mom. You're on top in the sex department. *Sex in America* says so. "The first surprise in our data was how little sex with a partner most people had: Only one-third of Americans aged eighteen to fifty-nine have sex with a partner as often as twice a week. We found that Americans fall into three groups. About a third have sex with a partner at least twice a week, a third have sex with a partner a few times a month, and the rest have sex with a partner a few times a year or have no sexual partners at all."

And the monogamous have the most chance of the most sex. It's easier for us. "A single person has to find someone, go on a date, go to dinner, get to know the partner. If and when they agree to have sex, then they both have to make time to have it, and drive to her house or his house," says Edward O. Laumann, a professor of sociology at the university and one of the authors of the study.

If one or both have kids, the arrangement is even more complicated.

Two sex partners does not mean you get twice as much sex. You may get twice as many complications. "You have to make time, make arrangements, and make sure your partners don't run into each other," Laumann says. "Married people don't have to worry about those things. They use that time to have sex."

That's why people who are having affairs often don't have

as much sex as monogamous couples. They have the problems of courtship, with a twist. "People in adulterous relationships report low levels of satisfaction. They describe
themselves with negatives. They report feeling shameful and
guilty," Laumann says.

There's a reason. "The majority of Americans still disapprove of adultery."

The National Health and Social Life Survey is everything
a monogamous person could want in a sex survey. And what
a survey. It was unquestionably scientific. It was faithful and
reliable. It was a survey we could believe in. A survey we
could live with—forever. It said what monogamous people
have longed to hear since Kinsey first came . . . er, burst . . .
no, I mean appeared on the scene almost fifty years ago:
We're sexier than single people. We do it more. We do it
better. We like it. Monogamous sex is more satisfying and
orgasmic.

This survey should have ended the shame of monogamy
once and for all: Monogamy is sexually superior. We could
finally put the myth of Ozzie and Harriet to bed—and in a
king-size bed, at that. But we didn't.

The survey was not heralded for its findings on
monogamy. It was sneered at. I told you what the newspaper said in St. Louis, which is the most monogamous city I
know: "'Heavy Sex?' Survey Finds Little of It—Faithfulness
the Rule; Obsession the Exception."

"S-E-X in the U.S.A.: Wake Us When It's Over," yawned
Ms. magazine.

A *Washington Post* commentary whined, "The Decline
and Fall of Fast and Loose: Wasn't Life More Fun When We
Imagined We Were Easy and Sleazy?"

Well, no. That was the point of the survey. We only imagined it. We really weren't getting much when we were single.

Never mind that the Chicago sex statistics were similar to other well-conducted surveys. We can't give up the idea that Americans are awfully wedded. We boomers have reexamined the roles of women. We've taken another look at men. We've changed our ideas about child rearing. But when it comes to marriage, we're still trapped in the fifties. Our view of monogamy comes straight out of sitcoms and *Playboy*. The wife is the old ball and chain. The husband is a gelded slob. There are only two ways to have exciting sex: Stay single or marry and have it on the sly. In this mythology, married sex is as much fun as flossing.

We're addicted to the surveys that support this myth.

Edward Laumann, the University of Chicago researcher, came to this conclusion. "The more outrageous a survey is, the more it's news. But the distortion from junk statistics does damage. Everyone overdoses on data and no one pays attention to what's going on."

But I did pay attention to what was going on that summer in my subdivision. It seemed like everyone was slipping around. How does the Chicago sex survey explain that?

Easy. There were at least two hundred families in that neighborhood. And how many cases of adultery? Three, maybe four, at the most. A few illicit lovers were gaudy enough to make it seem like everyone was doing it. Actually, more than 80 percent of the families were monogamous that year.

My subdivision was safely inside the Chicago survey's statistics.

And now that I look back, most of the bed hopping didn't last long. The outbreak of adultery could be blamed on many things: a marriage cracking because a workaholic spouse was never home or a woman sick with worry over an ailing relative who found some extracurricular comfort for a few weeks. Plus chronic alcoholism, semilethal loneliness, and male and female menopause.

So far as I know, only one person made a habit of adultery. The rest were going through a bad time. Then they quietly resumed their faithful lives.

If you look at it that way, monogamy was rampant in my neighborhood. Except for a few noisy interludes of adultery.

Of course, I don't really know what happened to all the people involved. The details were between them and their priest. And Father never told any secrets of the confessional.

Not even when he hung up his cassock and married that nice woman.

CHAPTER 3
Weddings Are What's Wrong With Monogamy

I was in the downtown bridal shop, getting fitted for my wedding dress. The shop advertised the lowest prices in the city on wedding dresses. I could see they weren't wasting any money on the decor. The wedding dress in the window looked like the model Miss Havisham wore in *Great Expectations*. It was older than I was and covered with dust. The display veil looked like a spiderweb. Inside, the shop was furnished with plain pipe racks and cheap mirrors that made thin women look gaunt and healthy women look like they were carved out of lard. The floor was covered with a carpet that I suspected didn't start out as gray. Over the dirty-gray carpet was a thick layer of threads shed from hundreds of altered bridesmaids' dresses. Peach seemed to be the big color this year. Every time I moved, I crushed imitation pearls and iridescent sequins into the carpet.

A woman who looked like Butterfly McQueen was altering my wedding dress. I'd seen *Gone with the Wind* four times, and I could have picked her out of any lineup. Butterfly knew this was a hurry-up job. I was getting married August sixth, and it was the end of July. She let out the sleeves and pinned the hem on my wedding dress. Then she took her finger and jabbed me hard, right in the gut. "You're not pregnant," Butterfly said, sounding surprised.

I didn't know about the prices, but the service here was definitely discount. I was pretty sure a seamstress at Saks wouldn't have tried this country pregnancy test. Butterfly had been feeling for my uterus. I was shocked. I was also stupid.

"Of course I'm not pregnant," I said. "I'm not married."

"Most brides are," said Butterfly, who knew being unmarried was not a contraceptive.

"I told you so," said my mother, who started crying again. "That's what everyone is going to think. They're going to think you had to get married."

A "premature" baby is no disgrace anymore. Most parents are grateful if the couple marries at all. Guessing the baby's true age provides hours of harmless fun for people who like to count backward on their fingers. But in 1972, in the very Catholic suburb of Florissant, this was still a terrible scandal. I didn't see what the problem was. I wasn't pregnant. In a few more months, when I wasn't waddling around in maternity clothes, everyone would figure that out.

Meanwhile, Don and I wanted to get married for the most romantic reason: We couldn't live without each other. Moving in together was not done in Florissant in those days. This was a tough blue collar area. Fathers worked at the Ford plant or in construction. They did not use shotguns on their daughter's defiler. They broke the guy's neck with their bare hands. So we decided to get married. Then I would go to the University of Missouri at Columbia and finish my last year of journalism school, and Don would teach English 115 at the St. Louis campus. We would live 120 miles apart during the week. We would see each other on the weekends, which would start about Wednesday. We would screw our brains out.

Don and I decided in May that we wanted to get married the first week of August. That would give us two weeks for a honeymoon before school. We had three months to plan the wedding. We thought we'd settled everything nicely. But the family was in an uproar. That's when we learned the first lesson: Weddings are what's wrong with monogamy.

The average wedding is about as romantic as root canal. Especially if you're a young bride, still living at home. If we could eliminate these whited spectacles, monogamy would have renewed respect. It would no longer be regarded as a joke.

Ideally, the wedding should be planned by the bride and the groom together. After all, a marriage is not a sacred ceremony between the bride and her mother. All too often, though, the bewildered groom backs away from the planning. His escape is approved by culture and custom. Women are supposed to be naturally interested in weddings. Men are not. There are racks of magazines for brides, but I've never seen one called *Groom*.

If you're a bride, the worst thing you can do is believe the people who say, "This is your day." Then you will have the mistaken idea that you are the focus of your wedding. Wrong. Your wedding is not about you. It's the last chance for your mother to have the wedding she wanted. After all, her wedding was for *her* mother.

It's also her last chance to fight with you. After the wedding, that privilege goes to the groom.

You and your mother will fight continually while you plan your wedding, even if you usually get along. Don't feel guilty. Simply accept it as another wedding tradition. Then the important question becomes where to hold the main fight. For brides who want an intimate affair, there's no place like home. Start three hours before the wedding, so the whole family can join in. Other brides prefer a large bash. In that case, the best place is the bridal shop. If there are lots of strangers around, this is a good time to announce you are pregnant.

No matter when you decide to marry, it will be the wrong time. Even if you give your parents a full year, you will still be wrong. Valentine's Day may sound romantic to you. Your mother knows better. That's when hotel and catering prices go up because dozens of other brides want the same date. If you want to be a June bride, your mother will have to fight fifty-five other mothers for the one acceptable place to hold the wedding. If you choose an off-peak time, like January, that's when the hotel closes and the good caterer goes on vacation.

My mother was furious that we couldn't get a good hall on short notice. To her, a good hall meant the VFW hall in Florissant, instead of the one fifteen minutes away in Berkeley. Only a mother could tell the difference. In our social circle, you had your reception at either the VFW hall or the American Legion hall. Guests sat at long folding tables covered with white paper and pitchers of Busch beer. The decorations were white paper bells and crepe paper streamers. The reception line was next to the turkey shoot posters. The band was six guys in iridescent green tuxes who played polkas and "Proud Mary." The menu was always the same: roast beef and ham on dollar rolls, two kinds of potato salad, and mostaccioli, an Italian noodle dish served by Germans and other ethnic groups at weddings because it feeds a lot of people on the cheap.

Your mother may also have a tremendous battle with your future mother-in-law over what color dress to wear. Mother-of-the-bride dresses look like shrouds with matching sleeveless coats. They come in two colors, blue and pink.

Both mothers will want blue. My mother won. She'd been toughened by fights with me, the florist, the caterer, and the photographer. She rolled over Don's mother like a tank. It was the last time the two women talked, except for a frigid "How do you do?" when they met formally at the rehearsal dinner.

When you are not at war with your mother, you will be facing some other crisis. One of your bridesmaids will almost certainly hate the dress you choose for her. She won't say it, but she suspects you've chosen it because you want her to look bad. She will never trust you again. That's not what is happening. Big church weddings have a maid of honor. But they also have the One Bridesmaid who stands out— because she looks so bad. The dress makes her look horrible because it is designed for the majority. If all the other brides- maids are thin, she is the one who's fat. If they're tall, she's short. If they're in scoop necks, she's concave and they're convex. Or vice versa. This doesn't happen to men. They all look about the same in a tux. But the bridesmaids' dress always looks ugly on one woman.

I was the One Bridesmaid once. I'm six feet tall. My friend the bride was about five feet tall. So was the groom. They looked so cute together. I never stopped to think that short people come from short families. And they would all be in the wedding. It gave new meaning to the phrase "small wedding."

For the One Bridesmaid, the trouble starts at the bridal shop. Bridesmaids' dresses are chosen by a democratic process. We vote on the style we like best. I knew I was in trouble when I showed up at the shop. If you stacked the whole wedding party, they wouldn't reach the ceiling. It was going to be five against one. Even worse, the other five women were wearing ruffles and lace. Like most tall people,

I prefer straight, simple lines. Imagine Sigourney Weaver in ruffles. Imagine me in misery. I looked at all the bridesmaids' dresses and voted for the simplest long thing I saw. The dressing room curtains. They were a stylish gray.

I was outvoted. The other bridesmaids wanted pink ruffled chiffon with lace jackets that stopped under the armpits. They looked dainty. I looked like a linebacker in lace shoulder pads. The dress cost me ten dollars more than the other women because I needed an extra-long skirt. I told myself it was only one day and it was just a dress. It didn't look that bad.

On the wedding day, I got up the courage to look in the mirror. There I stood, looking stupid in pink and lace. The ruffled V neck made my collarbones stick out more than my breasts. The lace jacket showed my Nautilus-sculpted arm muscles to perfection. The high waist made me look even taller. The dyed-to-match high heels wobbled.

When my husband Don saw me, he tried to reassure me. He said I didn't look like a linebacker. I looked like a road company *La Cage aux Folles*. At least, he tried to tell me. He was laughing so hard, he cried. He told me he always cried at weddings.

The One Bridesmaid is not your only crisis. You will have more. No matter how hard you try, one of your wedding invitations will go astray in the mail. And it will always be the one for your evil-tempered aunt. She will be sure you did it on purpose and cause a tremendous flap. Take comfort in this. It could be worse. In the old days, she would have turned you into a frog.

Then there is the problem of the bridal registry. Brides used to ask for the most expensive china, crystal, and silver patterns. Whole families would club together to buy the bride a butter knife. Twelve years later, when her youngest child drops the butter knife down the garbage disposal, she can't afford a new one.

I got married when the spirit of the sixties prevailed, so naturally I despised this money-grubbing practice. I didn't want a bridal registry. I wasn't going to tell wedding guests what to get me. I gave them the freedom to buy what they wanted. Ninety percent of the guests were friends of my parents and relatives who hadn't seen me since the family picnic fifteen years ago. They didn't have a clue. I wound up with sixteen ice buckets, fourteen bun warmers, six electric blankets, and twelve blenders. A bun warmer, for those with filthy minds, is an electric tray that keeps rolls warm. It is probably the most useless appliance ever devised, even worse than a fondue pot. I got seven of those. Plus some very odd gifts, including a Catholic sick call set so the priest could give us the last rites for the dead at home. We were supposed to hang it over our bed.

Duplicate wedding gifts that couldn't be returned, such as blenders, bun warmers, and ice buckets, made excellent wedding presents when my friends got married. But some presents were too ugly to pass on. The winner at my wedding was a set of gold fruit spoons, covered with warts. The warts turned out to be plums and pineapples. We did not despise these homely gifts. We pawned them to buy useful household items, such as six-packs and pizzas.

Today's brides have yet another option for a family fight. They can choose a sensible bridal registry. This means the bride registers at the hardware store, the Target store, or some other plebeian place for wedding gifts such as garden hoses, barbecue pits, and big-screen TVs. Expect mothers and/or aunts to be suitably shocked and deliver lectures like these: "Grandmother gave me her cut-glass and silver wedding gifts. What will you give your daughter? A set of socket wrenches?"

Maybe. And I'll bet she will use them more than Mom used that cut-glass pickle dish.

Just about the time there is a lull in the family fighting, the bride faces a new embarrassment—the shower. No matter how sophisticated you think you are, your friends or relatives will have one of these horrors in your honor.

A few enlightened people try to spread the embarrassment equally by holding a couple's shower. But most showers are still for the bride. Fortunately, the bridal shower is changing. Any woman is pleased to see the awful sexist ceremony of the bridal shower replaced by something more mature—like an evening of drinks and male strippers.

But before the bridal shower disappears completely, we should know what we are throwing away. A bridal shower answered certain ancient needs. It is the first chance to meet the new in-laws. And hold them up for loot. I consulted my city etiquette expert, Janet Smith, on the art of the traditional shower. According to Janet, the bridal shower needs these key elements:

First, the shower must be a surprise. This is difficult. The modern bride is crafty. "Often the family has to set up two or three events that look like surprise showers, before they spring the actual shower," Janet says. "One poor bride thought she was going to a Tupperware party. She wanted to return some bad Tupperware. The video camera caught her trying to stash a burpable bowl behind her back."

A bridal shower needs the right food. In the past, it was always cake and punch. Now, it's turning into a full meal: ham, tuna, or chicken salad. The chicken salad is often land mined with grapes, pineapple, or walnuts. The shower also has to have a decorated cake and a cute punch, which nobody drinks. A proper punch contains one or more of the following: lime sherbet, cheap champagne, Jell-O, pineapple juice. If you really want to get fancy, float some strawberries on top.

At the shower, at least one member of the family will not be speaking to another. They will exchange curt nods, and pointedly avoid each other, unless you spiked the punch. A shower is a chance for new feuds. Someone is sure to be offended when a bride's relative calls the groom "what's his name."

Since this is the first meeting for most of the family, all the best clothes come out. Guests also bring out their best manners. The veneer of civilization lasts until the games. Shower games have been blamed for the high rate of unmarried women. They are revolting. But no shower is complete without them. The dignified facade dissolves under the pressure of that shower favorite, Rob Your Neighbor. Guests roll dice for wrapped presents, usually bought at the Dollar Store. The presents keep changing hands until time runs out. Sweet-faced grandmothers will kill for a tea strainer. Top game presents include pot holders and big plastic hangers. These earn the highest shower compliment: "a lovely gift."

Speaking of gifts, shower presents are used to judge the generosity of the in-laws. The bride's mother gets high marks if she gives queen-sized sheets. This is a direct challenge to the groom's mother. There's also the traditional sniping between the relatives who give frivolous gifts and the ones who come up with Corning Ware.

During the gift giving, someone is sure to embarrass the bride with a honeymoon pack. The pack includes a small bottle of champagne, a deck of cards, a bottle of aspirin, and a flimsy nightgown labeled "in case of fire."

At the shower, one daughter has been delegated to smother the Aunt Who Will Say Anything—before she does. You can spot this aunt. Her clothes are as loud as she is. She usually wears rhinestones or gold lamé. The new in-laws would be shocked by what she blurts out—if they weren't trying to shut up their own aunt.

The wedding plans, the parties, and the showers seem to overwhelm an engaged couple. But there is also the spiritual side. You must have at least one fight with your minister.

Often, it starts when a young bride has an old-fashioned dream—and a minister has an old-fashioned rule. Many brides dream of walking down the aisle to the Wedding March. As little girls, they played dress up with the family curtains, pretending to march down the aisle to that traditional song. But some of them won't get their wish.

You know why?

There are churches that ban the Wedding March. They say it doesn't belong in a place of religion. Some people believe it's because the Wedding March was parodied in a dirty movie.

The problem is older than movies and more high-toned. The Wedding March is from an opera bedroom scene. The same name is used for two pieces of nineteenth-century music. You probably know the one as "Here Comes the Bride." It's the "Bridal Chorus" from Wagner's opera *Lohengrin.* The chorus serenades the bride in her bedroom.

Today, most brides are innocent of any knowledge of *Lohengrin.* Wagner is better known for driving modern listeners mad with boredom, not lust.

The traditional recessional piece is the Wedding March from Mendelssohn's incidental music to *A Midsummer Night's Dream.* Both Wedding Marches became hot stuff after Queen Victoria's daughter had them at her wedding in 1858. That union gave the world Kaiser Wilhelm — and World War I.

For more than one hundred years, these Wedding

Marches have been played for brides. But they were not conceived for churches. That leaves some pastors with an unhappy duty: They must break the news to a young bride with her heart set on that music. The brides are mostly Catholic and Missouri-Synod Lutheran. Some pastors allow the march. Some don't. No bride understands why. A Catholic bride says wistfully, "I wanted the Wedding March. The pastor told me no. I was eighteen. I didn't question him. I wished I had."

It wouldn't have done any good. A Lutheran bride got this reason: "My pastor said it was secular music and didn't belong at the service." She wasn't convinced. "When you think of getting married, you think of marching down the aisle to 'Here Comes the Bride.' It's weird not to have it at my wedding. It just doesn't seem right."

It seems very right to the pastors who make the rules. A Catholic monsignor told me that music at church should be of a clear religious nature. The couple should save the secular music for the reception. Some strict priests believe that Wagner's chorus is worse than secular; it's boudoir music. The bride is led to bed. It doesn't belong in church.

Disappointed brides can be tearful. How does this monsignor handle them? "Not too well," he confessed.

Of course, the bride could shop around. The pastor of the groom's church might allow the Wedding March. If the pastor permits the Wedding March, the bride may still have to persuade the church organist. One says she'll play it if the bride insists. "But it's hackneyed. It makes me think of that song I sang as a kid. You know it." Then the organist began the familiar words: "Here comes the bride, short, fat, and wide."

I remembered the rest of the song: "See how she waddles, from side to side."

Other couples have problems when it's time to face the music. They have to stand up in church and publicly declare their love. And that's where boomers have trouble. We boldly took charge of our wedding ceremonies in the sixties. We wrote our own invitations. I was invited to one wedding to "watch the coming together" of Sandy and Jim. I couldn't wait to see that. Turned out they were only getting married. The consummation took place in private.

We also wrote our own vows. The first word I wrote out of mine was a four-letter one, "obey." But however boldly we changed the wedding ceremony, there is one word we boomers won't say. It's funny because we're usually fearless about strong language. And our parents weren't afraid to use it. They said this five-letter word in church, in front of God and everybody.

I'm talking about the D word—Death, as in "till death do us part."

This phrase is traditional in many wedding ceremonies. But boomers don't like the word death in our marriage vows. It scares us to . . . er, we're mortally afraid of the subject. At least, that's what one Methodist minister believes. The Reverend Scott Lohse has married hundreds of boomers, many for the second time. "Boomers want to change their wedding vows to 'for as long as we both shall live' or 'all of our lives together,'" he says.

"Generation Xers don't mind the D word, and neither do their grandparents. They're happy to get married till death do them part. But boomers look for ways around it."

The Reverend Scott says one boomer bride found she couldn't look at death. She was married in a picture-pretty suburban church with a white steeple, green lawns, and an old-fashioned churchyard. "The bride burst into uncontrollable fits of laughter every time I mentioned 'till death do us part.' I finally asked her what was so funny. She could see the churchyard from where she stood. The bride says, 'I'm looking over his shoulder, and I see all those tombstones.'"

That look at the future made her nervous.

Other boomers are afraid of the past. "Some are folks who have been married more than once. They promised to do it forever the first time, and it didn't work out. They don't want to break another promise."

For a second or third marriage, they try to make vows they can honor. "They like 'all of our lives together.' If you think about it, that means they could divorce tomorrow. Their lives together may last one day or a lot longer."

Maybe even until death do them part.

Boomers also aren't big on sharing. "The ring ceremony says, 'I honor you with all that I am and all that I have.' They don't want to say that, either. I'm sorry to say it's men more often than women."

A guy may be eager to give himself in marriage. But he feels his new bride should be satisfied with this treasure. He's not about to unload the gold, too. "What most of these men really want to say is, 'All that I am and one-third of what I have after taxes,'" the Reverend Scott says.

Made sense to me. What's the point of having your lawyers work out a prenuptial agreement if you're going to stand up in front of witnesses and say you're giving her everything? It could cause problems later, when you divorce.

"I don't usually change that part. I think that's important. Marriage requires a level of trust. If they're not ready to share their worldly goods, they don't really want to marry again."

Still, the Reverend Scott admires his skittish and skeptical boomers. "They question authority, and I like that. The younger couples are very traditional. They seem to accept everything. They don't care what they say. They want a wedding just like Erica's on *All My Children*. Boomers want to shop for the best of everything, including the right vows."

We boomers don't mind saying we'll spend forever with the one we love. But we're not dying to do it.

Mike McCarthy is one exception. This man lives to get married. At age thirty-five, he's been married twice. He wants to get married fifty times—to the same woman.

"Our goal is to get married in every state," Mike says.

Mike was living in Hollywood when he met Ellyn McManus. They met cute, as they say out there.

"I was doing volunteer work at a radio station in LA," says Ellyn. "He called to request a song for a progressive rock show. We started talking because I was bored. We were on the phone for forty-five minutes. He gave me his number. The next time, I called him. We talked three hours. We decided to meet. I said he should bring a carnation, just to be cliche. He brought a can of Carnation condensed milk."

"I'm so thankful I met Ellyn," says Mike. "In a three-year period I dated one hundred women, all actresses."

Some were desperate to get married, although Mike wasn't sure that they wanted to commit monogamy. "One told me she was from South Africa and had married a homosexual to get a green card. On our first (and only) date, she stopped to make a pickup for a drug deal."

She made this charming proposal: "Want to have sex and get married so I can keep my green card?" I asked what happened to her husband. She said, "He died of AIDS."

Ellyn dated her share of losers, too. We can skip the depressing details and get to the good part. Ellyn and Mike were wildly in love. They wanted to marry. And that's when Ellyn discovered what many women find out too late: Her groom was hopelessly romantic. He wanted a big wedding.

"Ellyn wanted to do it in Vegas," Mike says. "She thought

we could save all the money and put it on a down payment for a house. But I'm a guy who truly looked forward to his wedding day."

Ellyn's mother was thrilled. Ellyn wasn't so sure, but she went through with it. "I had six bridesmaids, two flowers girls, and a big reception."

That was June 5, 1993. Six months later, Mike and Ellyn did it again. In December they got married in Las Vegas. "We had the wedding I wanted the first time," says Ellyn. It was cheap, in all senses of the word.

They were married at the Little White Chapel. The chapel was decorated with pictures of all the celebrities who'd blessed it: Jon Bon Jovi showed up there for a wedding of a band member, and the chapel arranged the ceremony for Demi and Bruce.

"The whole day was tacky," says Ellyn cheerfully. "We took the bus downtown to get the license. Our wedding breakfast was a free one-pound hot dog at the Lady Luck hotel. We got married in a little gazebo carpeted with Astroturf. We had on jeans and sunglasses. The minister not only gave the name of the chapel during the ceremony, but also announced the complete address with the ZIP code."

It sounds romantic.

"It was," says Ellyn.

"It brought tears to my eyes," says Mike. "It was just as moving the second time."

For this couple, weddings were becoming habit forming.

"We enjoyed them," says Mike. "We wanted more."

Next they decided to wed in St. Louis. They were going there to meet their two-year-old nephew. "We wanted to be married under the Arch, but the priest said no. This would be a serious wedding, even if it was the third time. He said we had to marry in the church."

Now they were dealing with the Midwest, where people still had standards. Mike worried that the third try in St. Louis might be trouble. He says he called a clerk in the St. Louis City Hall and explained the situation. "She says, 'I see. Oh, well, no problem, honey, no problem at all.' She said it sounded like fun. We should just come in and bring forty-seven dollars in cash for a license. Unfortunately, I didn't get her name.

"When we came to St. Louis, I called City Hall again. This time, I got another clerk. She says, 'No, you can't do that. She's wrong. What's your name?' I hung up."

Were Mike's intentions honorable? Or were he and Ellyn doing something illegal when they wanted to commit triple monogamy? I was so fascinated by their problem, I called the Missouri attorney general for an opinion. A spokesman says there seems to be nothing on the books preventing multiple monogamy with the same woman.

Sharon Carpenter, the St. Louis recorder of deeds, says Mike could have done the deed if he'd kept quiet. "Basically, we say no because Missouri recognizes marriages from all fifty states. I suspect when he tries to get married elsewhere, other states will tell him the same thing. If he's smart, he'll keep his mouth shut. My advice is to go in and play like it's the first time."

So what did the couple do when their third wedding was unceremoniously canceled?

"We had lunch with the priest," says Ellyn.

Mike and Ellyn have vowed to continue marrying in every state. Seattle, Washington, is their next target. They may even sneak back to St. Louis for another attempt at monogamy.

"My ideal marriage is to lay down in Four Corners, where four states meet—Arizona, New Mexico, Utah, and Colorado—and have four different kinds of ceremonies—maybe Catholic, Jewish, Protestant, and Buddhist," Mike says.

"That's exotic."

"It's also economy," he says. "Four states at once."

"Why get married again and again? Once is enough for most people."

"To be different," Ellyn says. "I don't have a spoon collection. I have marriage licenses."

"I'm hoping all these weddings will make it a hell of a lot harder to get divorced," says Mike.

For Better or Worse

Monogamy isn't about living together. Any two reasonable people can live together for a while, as long as one of them doesn't use all the hot water.

The real test of monogamy is, Do you want to die with this person?

One of my steady dates failed this test. Jim and I had been going out for over a year. He was ambitious, smart, and good-looking. He had a cute little-boy cowlick and big brown eyes.

Everyone, including me, thought we'd get married when Jim graduated. We had so much in common. We both liked 1965 Mustangs, Beatles music, and *Laugh-In*.

It's true that Jim had an irritating snort-giggle. Also, his habit of slurping my lip when we kissed made me shudder, and not with delight. But I figured once we got married and got around to doing the big stuff, little problems like these would work themselves out.

Then I was in a car accident and caught some weird infection at the hospital. I lost almost twenty pounds. My teeth bothered me, too. I went to the dentist one Friday. The dentist poked around in my mouth and then said he wanted to talk to me in his office.

I stumbled into one of his red leather wing chairs. He was sitting in front of a wall of books, looking as trustworthy as a doctor in an aspirin commercial. He had a fat medical book open on his desk.

"I've made some tests," he said solemnly. "I won't get the results back until Monday. But I'm certain you have leukemia."

Gaack! Forget the hopeful talk and the survival statistics. I was going to die at age twenty. This was when *Love Story* had the nation in its sappy grip. Everyone was weeping over the deathbed scene of the girl who loved Beethoven, Bach, and the Beatles. She died a lingering death. From the same thing the doctor said I had.

I could see myself in Ali MacGraw's hospital room. It would be filled with roses. It would not be filled with disgusting things like IV tubes and urine bags. My gown would not flap open in the back and my hair would be freshly washed and curled. As the end drew near, Ryan O'Neal would take me into his arms and kiss me to death.

Except it wouldn't be Ryan O'Neal. It would be Jim. The last thing I would feel would be Jim slurping my lip like a Popsicle. The last thing I would hear would be him giggling and snorting. He always did that when he was nervous. I didn't want to leave this world with him going "Heh-heh-heh, snort."

No thanks. I'd rather die alone.

I bounced Jim that Saturday night. On Monday, the dentist told me I didn't have leukemia. I also didn't have a steady date anymore.

But I knew I'd made the right decision when I dumped Jim. I'd broken the news as we sat in his Mustang in the Steak N Shake parking lot, eating Steakburgers and fries. I gave him a tearful parting speech: "I don't love you any more," I said, "but we can always be friends."

I expected Jim to sob brokenly. I would say it was better for both of us this way. He would say he'd always remember me. I would mope around for a few days, unable to eat. Then I would look good in my swimsuit when I started checking out cute guys at the Florissant pool.

Unfortunately, Jim took me literally about the "just friends" part. He gulped and snorted a few times. He looked sad. Then he said, "Listen, I know it's over. But I bought these two tickets to the play tonight, and I don't want to waste them. You wanna go anyway?"

The man had no soul. How could I live with him when I didn't want to die with him?

Now, Don was different. This was a man I could die with. In fact, I almost did on our second date. Don and I both loved beer dives and grease joints. We were going to a riverfront bar in Hardin, Illinois, that had cold steins of beer and the best fried catfish in a three-state flood plain. I still remember the crust, light yet crunchy.

I don't remember what we talked about. We were so dazzled by each other, it was like being drunk. I thought he was the smartest, funniest man I'd ever met. In between talking about everything, we gave each other hungrier looks than we gave the catfish.

It was dark by the time we walked out the door, holding hands. We found Don's car parked among the Hardin Harleys and started the drive back to St. Louis on those twisty country roads. On a dark and deserted stretch, the power-steering belt broke. It was an S curve. Don steered his heavy Plymouth VIP through one curve, but on the second curve the car slid across the road and went right through the wooden barrier. It snapped like one of those balsa-wood model planes. The barrier was so flimsy, I wondered why they'd bothered to put it up. The car bounced down the embankment, hitting rocks and branches and finally a tree.

Strangely, the destructive ride down was fun. I remember thinking, as the car rocked and rolled, the windows smashed, and the safety glass swirled around us, that it was a shame our families were going to be upset when they found our bodies because this didn't hurt at all. Then we landed on the tree. There was an ugly CRAK! That was the sound of Don's leg breaking. His leg was crushed between the bashed-in door and the steering column. My arms and knees were covered with blood and cuts from the window glass and the dashboard toggle switches, but I didn't feel anything. Except happy. I'd found a great man, and he was trapped in the car and couldn't get away. I climbed up that hill in high heels as if they were hiking boots. Then I hung onto a road sign and flagged down a van full of real sixties hippies.

Two of them drove off for help. The ones who stayed behind offered more help. "You wanna toke?" they asked. I turned them down. I was already high. While they waited for the police, the ambulance, and the wrecker, I went back down the hill and proposed to Don.

"Now that I've got you where you can't get away," I began. "Will you marry me?"

"Do you really want to marry a broken-down English teacher?" he asked, already dazed.

"No, I want to marry you, the smartest, funniest man I ever met."

A good kisser, too. Don didn't suck on my lip like a breath mint. We spent the rest of the wait kissing the blood off each other. It had a warm, salty taste that was better than any champagne. *Love Story* really gave dying a bad name.

Of course, neither one of us died. Don had the most serious injuries. He spent weeks in the hospital and the rest of the hot summer in a plaster cast from his waist to his toes. I got some eighty-seven stitches in the emergency room and went home. The next day, I felt as fried as the catfish. I was cut, bruised, and sore. I also had a bad case of cold feet. I was horrified that I'd proposed to Don. No lady proposes to a man, I decided, turning suddenly Victorian in 1971.

I called Don at the hospital and rescinded the proposal. Fortunately, he showed he had the right qualities to survive long-term monogamy. He knew when to ignore me. As soon as he got out of the hospital, he got his friend Charlie to drive him to my parents' house. Don showed up at the front door in a wheelchair. He was wearing a white shirt, my favorite blue jacket, and a pair of pants slit all the way to the crotch on the side of his bad leg. The pants were held together with strips of elastic to accommodate the cast. Just in case the elastic slipped at some crucial moment, Don had stuffed a clean white handkerchief at the top of the slit. Mother said a man who carried a clean handkerchief was a gentleman, and here was proof.

This time Don proposed to me, in his wheelchair, in my parents' living room. I cried. He said, "I'd offer you my handkerchief, but under the circumstances I need it more than you do."

After that, I would do anything for him, even go through a wedding. We were married in August, as soon as the doctor cut him out of the cast.

Our courtship was typical of most people who commit monogamy. Their stories aren't all cliffhangers, like ours. But they do have a legend to live by. Maybe it's how they first met or what happened when he proposed or what their best man did at their wedding. You can't commit monogamy without at least one special story.

Judith S. Wallerstein did a study of successful marriages. She found that these romantic memories were important for lasting marriages. "Happily married couples treasure these images and episodes," Wallerstein wrote in *The Good Marriage* with Sandra Blakeslee. "The story of how they met and courted is given special status and dignity, set apart from everyone else's history. Told again and again, the story reaffirms the couple's early pleasure and their present togetherness."

These romantic stories are a cushion for the rocky times that can erode your love—when he is grumping because he has to take out the garbage or when she is whining that she's sick of mopping the kitchen floor for ingrates who don't have the sense to take off their muddy shoes. Or vice versa—he's upset because she's tracked up his floor, and she's bitching that she took out the trash last time. It helps to remember your romance. It's a reminder that marriage means more than having sex with your roommate.

These stories are also the treasures you take out when your marriage seems heading for bankruptcy: When he hates your job. When you hate that he's out of work. When you can't agree how to handle your son, who flunked English. When you want a new house and your spouse says you can't afford a move. You remember them on the days when you want to forget you ever married.

Janet and Kevin Smith keep the reason they got married in the garage. They had a baby boomer romance. Janet says they would have never married if Kevin hadn't gone to Vietnam.

"We went to high school together, but he never dated me. He was a snob, a rich kid. His clothes were perfect. He had the right penny loafers and the right pants in exactly the right shade of beige. You know how perfect he dressed? In his sophomore year, he wore an ascot for his school picture. He wasn't going out with the likes of me, a nobody who lived on not-so-Grand Avenue.

"When he went to Vietnam, he asked everyone he knew to write him, including two girls in my group. Girls travel in groups, and we were all walking along when Kevin came up to us and said, 'I'm going in the service. Gonna write? Gonna write me?' He asked all the girls. Even me. I said, 'Yeah, sure.' I wrote him. I wrote four guys in Vietnam. I had the time. I had a long bus ride to work. I also sent brownies. I sent cookies once, but all he got were crumbs.

"I think what did it was the Christmas tree. I sent him a three-foot tree. It was a little fake one, green, with about ten branches you stuck in the trunk, and lights and garlands. It was the only Christmas tree for miles around in Vietnam. That's when Kevin asked me to wear his ring. I said no. I didn't want to be tied down. As I tell the kids, I didn't always look like this. I used to have long blonde hair with no gray. I used to run around with no bra. Those days are gone.

"Anyway, a year later, we were engaged. Kevin came back from Vietnam and brought that tree with him. We looked so young when we married. After the reception, we had reservations at a big hotel. We got to the hotel just as a high school prom was letting out. The desk clerk didn't believe we were just married. He thought we were high school kids. We told him we had reservations—but who believes reservations for Mr. and Mrs. Smith? The hotel wouldn't give us our bridal suite or the champagne Kevin ordered. We spent our wedding night in a dumpy little room."

Janet and Kevin now have three kids. He's a bus mechanic. She's a homemaker and PTA treasurer.

"I can't believe we're married almost twenty-five years. You do need the good stuff for the bad days. I think that's the only reason Kevin stayed with me sometimes, because we had such a good beginning. We still have the tree. And the ascot."

Judy was a teenage bride. No one thought her marriage would survive. "Not when you elope at sixteen," she says.

To understand why she married when she did, you have to picture the times: It was 1956 when Ron Taylor met Judy.

Eisenhower was running for his second term. Elvis sang "Heartbreak Hotel" and "Love Me Tender." The minimum wage was one dollar an hour. Cars had fins. Women did not have jobs, especially once they married. If they worked, everyone assumed their husbands were not good providers.

But most important, nice girls did not—I repeat—did not sleep with boys before marriage. Especially nice Catholic girls. In those days girls had reputations, which were lost faster than you lose umbrellas. A reputation could be lost just being seen in bad company. That was any boy who wore black leather or a DA (duck's ass) haircut. Forget what you've heard about the fabulous fifties. It was a buttoned-down time. Elvis was for greasers, and guys who looked like the Fonz were trash. If a girl was spotted coming out of a car with steamed-up windows, her reputation was lost. If she stayed out all night with a boy, even if they fell asleep in the car, her reputation was gone. It was kaput if she was in his room, no matter what the reason.

Once a girl lost her reputation, no man would ever marry her. She was damaged goods, unfit for the fifties marriage market. She would never find a man to take care of her.

Judy says, "It was drilled into us from birth, 'He won't buy the cow if the milk is free.'" It sounds revolting now, comparing women to cows, but in the fifties, everyone followed the herd. "We were told that, and we believed it."

Now that you understand what Judy and Ron Taylor faced, here is their story. "Ron came to my thirteenth birthday party," she says. "He crashed the party. He was seventeen. When he walked in, my friends said, 'Oh, that's Ron Taylor. All the girls in the school love Ron Taylor.'

"I said, 'There's something wrong with all the girls.' I didn't find him attractive at all. I'm five-two and he was extremely tall. He was six-three. That was a turnoff. He carried himself with authority, and I didn't like that, either. He walked very straight, shoulders back, head up. I wasn't impressed. I was a cheerleader and very popular. I was good in school and good at athletics.

"Ron came to my house all summer long. We talked. When I started high school, he was a senior. I only dated him out of spite, because all the other girls wanted him."

When did you fall in love?

"We broke up for my sophomore year in high school because I wanted to date other guys. Ron would come over to my house. I'd see him sitting there, talking to my father. We started dating again, right before my junior year. I thought he was kind, compassionate, and gentle.

"We were at the point where necking no longer satisfied us. I just couldn't cross that line and do that to my parents. We eloped. We went on a Saturday in March 1959. We ran away to Edwardsville, Illinois, about twenty miles from home, and lied about our age. We got married by a Justice of the Peace in the courthouse. My husband was twenty and I was sixteen. I wore a white lace sheath dress that I'd worn to a dance. I had a corsage. Ron wore a suit. We had matching wedding bands, but after the ceremony, we took them off.

"We spent Saturday night together at my sister's house. She knew. Then we went home on Sunday. My parents also knew we were married. His didn't. We couldn't tell anyone else. In that day and time, a girl couldn't go to school and be married. We didn't live together for a whole year. I went to school and he did, too. We saw each other every day. It was like we were dating. My mother still rode herd on us. I accepted that. We had curfews and rules like every other couple. We got together whenever we dated, in the back seat of the car or whatever. We always found a way.

"I was eighteen and a senior in high school when I graduated. I was six months pregnant. I was able to hide it. I was very small and didn't put on any weight. It was important to my father that I got that diploma."

Judy and Ron didn't live together until April 1960. "It was a good way to ease into marriage. By then we were used to each other. I was ready to be a homemaker. He had finished two years of college and started working."

Ron had a job with a lot of people under him. "He was a caretaker for a cemetery. When I was pregnant, we struggled along. We ate a lot of soup. I ate so much Campbell's that I thought I was going to barf. One Friday my mom called and said, 'I made a big pot of soup, come on over.' I couldn't face any more soup, even if it was free. I said, 'I think we'll pass, Mom.' "

After seven years, Ron and Judy were married by a priest. That set the final seal on the marriage for traditional Catholics. "It wasn't a big wedding. We were married in the priest's parlor and had a party afterward. There was a football game on TV that day, and the priest asked if he could marry us at halftime. We said, 'No problem, we're both football fans.' "

The wedding had a happy outcome.

"Mizzou won the game," she says.

Bonnie Lynn Colemire tried twice to marry Larry. "But I just couldn't go through with it. The preparations for a big wedding were overwhelming. Once, plans were so far along, we had to take back the bridesmaids' dresses and candle arrangements."

What finally convinced her to make the leap to monogamy?

"I am an avid coupon clipper. I got a coupon for 10 percent off on a wedding chapel."

It seemed only fair. Bonnie Lynn met Larry at church. A couple of church ladies introduced them when the Ohio woman was visiting Napa, California. They clicked like castanets.

"Pretty soon Larry and I were deep in conversation. The man who locked up the church began to flick the lights, which meant 'Come on, move it! I want to get home!' I told Larry that it was nice meeting him and added, 'I'll be at the church convention in Stockton before leaving for Ohio.' I hoped he would get the hint and meet me there. We really seemed to have a lot in common. I began to look forward to the convention, but regretted meeting Larry. I didn't want to start a long-distance relationship."

They fell in love at the convention. Then she left him. "I started the drive back to Ohio the next day. After about six days of driving and stopping at friends' houses, I arrived home to find flowers and a letter. We decided that we had to see each other again."

Bonnie Lynn went back to California for ten days. "After that visit, we called every day. Larry ended up getting his phone disconnected because his bill was too high. We talked about getting married, but I had cold feet. We tried to plan a wedding twice, but I always chickened out."

Bonnie Lynn moved to St. Louis. She had a chance to teach there. She also saw lots of Larry, thanks to an airfare war. But she still wouldn't commit matrimony.

"During spring break of 1993 I flew out to see Larry again. We had a wonderful week together. I was going back on Sunday, but I wanted to do research in Reno, a four-hour drive from Napa. Thursday morning Larry and I headed out to Reno with a pen and notebooks, nothing else. As we were leaving his mother and father joked, 'You two will probably get married out there!'

"While we drove we, too, joked about the idea of eloping. Pretty soon our joking became serious. We began asking questions like: Where would we live? Who has the better benefits at work? What would our parents say?

"I think we pretty much made up our minds by the time we got to Reno. I really wanted to do research, but my head was swimming and I was tired. We rented a motel room and went right to sleep. We woke feeling refreshed and certain about what we were going to do. But I didn't want to get married late in the evening, which it was by the time we had purchased our wedding rings and other necessities of life—like everything we failed to bring because we thought we would be returning to Napa that evening.

"The next morning, I saw a coupon for the Chapel of the Bells wedding place. I laughed out loud. I couldn't resist. I clip coupons for everything, and now I had one for my wedding chapel. How could life get any better?

"When we got to the chapel, we found that the minister was on call. Thank God they got the right pager number and the plumber didn't show up. The receptionist gently pushed us through the double-wide doors of the chapel. We walked down the aisle and ten minutes later we were married.

"On the plane back, I looked down at my ring and wondered what I had done. Larry put all his affairs in order and met me in St. Louis in less than a month. Now this is the happily-ever-after part: We have two kids and a house."

Their wedding story gets Larry and Bonnie Lynn through the lean times. "We were totally alone when we married. We said, 'If we can do this alone, we can do anything.' Whenever something bad hits, or we do something scary, like buying our house, we always say, if we can get married alone, we can do anything."

Laurie and Matt Dohse didn't want to deal with a big wedding, either. They tried the modern version of eloping. They had a "weddingmoon," a combination wedding and honeymoon. They ran off to Florida last year with twenty of their closest friends and relatives and got married on the beach at sunset.

"It was so romantic," says Laurie. "It was perfect."

Only one thing went wrong for this couple. Call it a question of size. This is the short story of Laurie's long couch.

Laurie is a city kid. Matt wanted to move to a small town. Laurie wasn't sure she could live in a place where the ground was covered with grass instead of concrete. After all, that grass grew in dirt. It just wasn't sanitary. There were no police sirens to lull her to sleep. The crickets bellowed all night long.

But Laurie loved Matt and agreed to try life in a small town. They would get an apartment first. If the move worked, they'd look for something more permanent. She did make a deal with Matt: If she got new furniture, he'd get a new town. They found a couch at a big warehouse store in the city.

The sofa showroom was bigger than Davenport, Iowa. Inside were enough couches for every shrink this side of Vienna. In a herd of couches, Laurie's looked normal sized, even small. Alone, it was a majestic expanse of soft mauve and gray, a small mountain range. It awed their friend Rick, who helped them pick it up at the warehouse. "Rick took one look and said, 'It's big.'"

At the new apartment, Laurie realized just how big it was.

"Rick and Matt couldn't get the couch up the stairs. They put a hole in the wall trying. It just stayed there, stuck on the stairs. I was stuck, too, at the top of the steps. I started crying. Matt couldn't even get to me. The couch was between us. I cried, 'I'm not moving here. It's an omen.'

"Rick said, 'Don't worry, Laurie. We'll get that couch in the apartment if we have to walk it up a ladder and put it through a window.'"

The couch wouldn't fit through the window, either. "Matt said, 'Laurie, we can't get the couch in anywhere. It has to go back.'"

Laurie didn't want to take the couch back. There was nothing wrong with it. She just had too much of a good thing. The couch was seven feet long and thirty-six inches wide.

"My mom was no help. She said, 'You bought a couch and didn't measure it?' It didn't look that big in the showroom."

Laurie remembered that her future mother-in-law had offered them a couch to use until they found one they liked. They loaded up their big couch and drove twenty miles to her almost in-laws' home. It was now 10:45 at night. Laurie left her never-been-sat-on couch with Matt's mother and took the old couch.

"I kept paying eighty-four dollars a month on a couch I didn't have. I visited it regularly all summer long. Every time I saw my mother-in-law, I would check out my couch. She offered to send me pictures."

Laurie didn't laugh.

She did like living in their new town. After their wed-dingmoon, she and Matt began looking for a house. "I told the real estate agent exactly what I wanted: Our home had to have a thirty-six-inch-wide door and a clear shot for a seven-foot couch."

She got it. "We measured everything in the house. All you have to do is make that mistake one time. After almost nine months, my couch made it home. It looks great."

It was a perfect fit in her new life.

CHAPTER 5
One Perfect Harley

I think the most humiliating day in my marriage was an infamous February fifteenth. It was the day after Valentine's Day, a dreaded day in monogamy.

The original Saint Valentine was beheaded. I'm not surprised. Men have been losing their heads on this day ever since. They have also been roasted, burnt, and given the cold shoulder. All because they fail to understand how much major monogamous holidays mean to women.

Men can be romantic every other day of the year. But if they forget Valentine's Day, women will brand them bums. Don't ask me why. We're just sentimental, I guess.

Don forgot Valentine's Day when we'd been married five years. I was twenty-six and worried. I'd found one gray hair already that year, and it was only February. I yanked the sucker out of my scalp, but it didn't help. I knew the frost of old age was closing in on my head. At least I had a hot romance to warm my heart. On Valentine's Day Don always showed how much he loved me.

I waited hopefully all day at work while delivery people came through the office carrying everything from red roses to potted palms—for other women. Well, that was fine with me. Don didn't go for crude displays. He had something more intimate in mind.

I sat through a dull dinner at home, waiting for him to whip out some surprise in pretty paper. By nine o'clock, I knew there was going to be a surprise, all right, but it would be an ugly one: nothing. I was miserable. He didn't love me anymore. If he did, he would have given me a card or a single red rose.

After all, this was the man who two years before gave me a single red Thunderbird. Last year, it was the perfect pair of gold earrings, tasteful yet sexy. For our second anniversary, he found a watch of such timeless beauty it still gets compliments twenty years later.

And this Valentine's Day . . . nothing.

I sobbed, my heart broken, my life turning as gray as my hair.

"You don't love me anymore. You didn't remember Valentine's Day. You didn't have to give me anything expensive—just one rose," I said sniveling pathetically, like the Little Match Girl.

Don paced up and down the room, hurt and puzzled, as if this argument was being conducted in Urdu and that's why he didn't understand a word.

"I forgot," he said, expecting me to be impressed by this manly admission.

I wasn't.

"It doesn't mean I don't love you," he said reasonably. "I've remembered every other holiday, birthday, and anniversary. I just forgot this one, that's all. I sent you a dozen red roses for your birthday. I sent them to your office, too."

He'd understood that a present is a trophy.

"Your birthday was nine days ago. All I do is buy presents, for Christmas, your birthday, and now Valentine's Day. They're too damn close together."

I erupted into more heartbroken sobs.

"It's not my fault I was born in February," I cried. "I hate it. It's always cold, and I never got any good birthday presents as a kid. People would hand me one present at Christmas and say, 'Here, it's big, it counts for both days.'"

Don looked stricken. He promised to make it up to me.

That's how February fifteenth became my day of shame. At 10:30 that morning I heard a buzz in the newsroom that seemed to be coming toward our department. A delivery man came staggering in under a flower arrangement that had to be four feet tall. It looked like something for a mob funeral. It was mostly spiky orange birds of paradise, along with other exotically ugly blooms in purple and red that looked like bath brushes and bulbous sex toys. In the center of this psychosexual nightmare was a gigantic Styrofoam cupid wearing a huge purple ribbon that said "Love." I was stunned by its grossness. I felt like Don had stuck his finger in my eye.

"Who sent that?" said an office troublemaker, a balding fat guy with a gut like a shoplifted kettle drum.

"Don," I said. My voice sounded strange and rusty. The single word stuck in my throat.

"Looks like he stole it off Jacqueline Susann's grave," Kettle Drum guffawed.

"Guess he showed you, huh?" said a ferret-faced subeditor, who instantly divined why I was getting flowers on February fifteenth. "Next year you'll be glad when he forgets Valentine's Day."

Half an hour later, Don called. "So what did you think?" he said, cheerfully.

"I think I never want to talk to you again," I said and hung up.

The insensitive clod had called up to gloat at my shame

and misery. I made some excuse to leave work early, taking the despicable flowers with me. I drove home, thinking about where I'd like to ram one particular weed that looked like a Roto-Rooter.

When I came in with the hideous heap of hell flowers, Don looked startled. Then he started laughing. He wrapped his arms around me, and the whole story came out.

Don felt so guilty about forgetting Valentine's Day that he went to a city florist, plunked down fifty pre-Carter-inflation dollars, and asked for "something spectacular." Unfortunately, the florist really did specialize in mob funerals, political dinners, and other events where you need to make a big impression fast. Their idea of spectacular went more for size than style.

Suddenly, the whole episode was funny. We'd survived the forgotten Valentine's Day. We even had a funny story to add to the family treasury of tales. But we both were tense and skittish around anniversaries and holidays for a long time after that. The easy, openhanded generosity was gone for several years. Gift giving became a duty, with horrific consequences if things went wrong. Don seemed afraid to buy things. He even asked me outright what I wanted. He looked hurt and unhappy when I said, "You used to know."

Finally, he asked, "Why are these holidays so important?"

It was a question I also asked myself. Why did I care so much? Why did other women act this way? I never saw a man burst into tears because his wife forgot their anniversary. Why are we women so hurt when our men forget some milestone of monogamy? It's more than simply missing out on a present. We aren't spoiled children.

The best answer is in a single sentence in *The Good Marriage* by Judith Wallerstein and Sandra Blakeslee.

"This is what toasts and flowers and anniversaries are

for—to celebrate us, our history, and, by logical extension, our future," these women wrote.

Only a woman would understand that statement. When her man forgets a major monogamous holiday, a woman wonders about the state of their union. She is angry and hurt because he is *not* celebrating their future. In fact, the two of them may not have a future. That's how much gifts mean to us.

Some women use bad presents as milestones marking the end of the road for their marriage. "I think the last gift from my ex was also the last straw that broke the back of our marriage," says Ashley. "I said I wanted something feminine for my birthday. I was thinking of perfume. He bought me a toy pink Cadillac."

Men hear this story and laugh. They think the guy had a sense of humor and Ashley was a spoilsport. Women understand. They know her husband refused to take her seriously. She was right to dump the joker. They know she chose wisely the second time around. Her husband-to-be tried to sell his antique Harley to "buy me a blinding rock for an engagement ring. It was mesmerizing. I wouldn't let him trade it for his Harley. There are only seventeen hundred of those in the world." He kept the Harley. She kept him and settled for a less expensive but more sentimental sapphire, "the symbol of romance and love."

Another female friend told me this story, in the hushed tones used for horrors: "The worst gift was the one George's brother gave his wife the first Christmas they were married—a .22-caliber rifle. She had an infant at the time. Can you imagine? I think it was cool that she didn't shoot him on the spot, but she did ditch him later."

Yes, the man remembered the holiday—but with something that was dead wrong for her. That awful gift was an early sign that the marriage was shot—at least to the women who heard the story. Many men wonder why she didn't at least try squirrel hunting before she gave him the boot.

Men don't understand why women make gift giving into a big deal. Women don't understand why men make gift giving into a big problem. A man has to remember only four days out of 365: your birthday, your wedding anniversary, Valentine's Day, and Christmas. Add one more, Mother's Day, if you have children. Is that so much?

For most men, the answer is yes. They shudder at the mention of shopping for Mother's Day. They work hard to forget Valentine's Day, the most flagrantly advertised love holiday in history. They regard buying a gift as one more unpleasant chore, like changing the oil or mowing the lawn.

Don summed up their pathetic excuses this way: "But I like to buy you presents when I feel like it, not because I have to."

"So why don't you feel like it on our anniversary?"

"It's so regimented," he said.

Regimented is the right word. It's total war if you forget, bud.

That is one main difference between men and women: Most men can't remember special occasions. Most women never forget them. I don't know why men have such a rough time remembering. Surely, the angry scenes their mothers had with their fathers are indelibly engraved in their minds.

Whole industries were built on men's forgetfulness. Remember the yellow candy boxes called Whitman's Samplers? About twenty-five years ago, they were marketed as a marital aid. The sole reason Whitman's Samplers used to be sold by the cash register at saloons and drug stores was to save marriages. In the olden days, most stores didn't stay open late. But a forgetful husband could always grab a box of candy at a drugstore or neighborhood bar. Finally, the sampler became identified with forgetfulness itself. I still remember my Aunt Sally bursting into tears when my Uncle Dan handed her a Whitman's Sampler on her anniversary. "Drugstore candy," she wailed. "You forgot again."

Some experts believe chronic male forgetters are former C students. To them, a holiday is just another test. Naturally, they flunk it. Another theory is that after a few years of being yelled at on Valentine's Day and their anniversary, men fail to associate these days with love and other tender feelings.

Freud wasn't the only man to ask, What do women really want?

The answer is, She's probably told you. You weren't listening.

The next question for most men is, What is a hint, and where can I get one?

Some women drop subtle hints. Men need to learn to recognize them. Here's a sample: "Instead of getting me that overpriced perfume I take back every year, Floyd, I'd rather have dinner at a nice restaurant."

That is a hint. So is this: "Margie got the most wonderful blouse for her birthday from her husband. It's powder blue, size ten, made by Frank of Festus, and it's on sale for $57.95. If it looks good on Margie, I know it would look good on me."

Some hints are meant to simply remind a man that an important day is coming up: "Forget Valentine's Day again this year, sweetheart, and I walk."

Getting the wrong gift is another problem. Some men are shopping impaired. These men always buy the wrong presents for the women they love. A shopping-impaired male would buy pajamas with feet for Madonna, and look hurt when she took them back. He thinks all black skirts are created equal and wonders why his wife didn't like the nice blender for her birthday after she complained the old one broke.

Shopping-impaired males do not deserve our scorn. With time, they can be educated. They may never be natural shoppers, but at least they will not feel so malled when an important monogamous holiday approaches. Treated with compassion, a shopping-impaired male can be a functioning member of the family. I've spent a lot of time working with the poor twits. They ask the same questions, over and over. Here are the five most common questions:

(1) **What's wrong with giving her money? A nice savings bond? Or a dreamy little Black & Decker power saw?**

Easy, sir. Let's take these questions one at a time. First, never give the woman you love money, unless she asks for it. If she wants you to leave the cash on the dresser, there may be something wrong with your relationship, but that's another question. And please don't tell her, "Money is always the right color and size." It doesn't take any thought to whip out your wallet. You pay employees, not your beloved. She needs a gift that shows you've thought of her. If you can't think of anything, give a gift certificate from her favorite store. It's as good as money, but takes more effort.

(2) **Doesn't a savings bond show some foresight?**

That kind of bonding is not romantic. It reduces your love to a financial transaction. Besides, why give her something else that won't mature for twenty years? She's already had to put up with you.

(3) **What's wrong with a Black & Decker power saw?**

Nothing, if she likes to build things in the basement. Otherwise, you're buying it for another loved one—yourself. Ditto for tickets to the hockey game. Unless she is a hockey fan, she won't light up like a scoreboard when you say, "I bought these for you so we could do something together."

(4) **I always ask the sales consultant for help. I tell her,**

"My wife's about your size." But my wife never likes anything I get. Do you know why?

Because your wife probably isn't her size. When I worked in a dress shop in college, fifty-year-old men said the same thing to me and I was pretty sure their wives weren't nineteen years old and six feet tall. What these men really meant was, "I'd like my wife to be about your size," which isn't the same thing.

Shopping is hard work. Liberated men must learn that standing around looking helpless won't buy it any more. Before you buy clothes for a woman, find out her size. Learn how she feels about elastic waistbands, stirrup pants, and synthetic fabrics. Know her favorite colors and her tastes in prints or plaids.

(5) Just before Christmas, the microwave broke, so I surprised my wife with a new one. She became very angry and told me what I could do with it, which would have voided the one-year warranty. What did I do wrong?

Buy appliances for your house, not for your wife. Running the household is a shared responsibility. Don't get her a microwave for Christmas unless you want a new steam iron for your birthday. Microwaves, steam irons, and SaladShooters are gifts that give monogamy a bad name. They enforce the idea that a monogamous woman is a housekeeper who has sex with her employer.

Worse, these gifts show no imagination. Did you give her a steam iron while you were courting? Did you sit on the sofa with her and say, "Look, my darling, it has settings from delicate to hot, just like my feelings for you!" If she didn't want a steam iron when she first fell in love with you, why do you think she'd want one now? No wonder people don't want to admit they're married.

That doesn't mean a woman won't hanker for something

hot and shiny—like a Harley. That's what Allison got for her twenty-fifth wedding anniversary: one perfect Harley.

And, no, her husband didn't get her a bike so he could use it. Bill doesn't ride. He's a golfer. But he does understand that "an anniversary gift should not have a cord and a warranty."

Bill is a former shopping-impaired male. Allison says his gifts used to be dreadful. "One year, he got me a set of knobby bike tires and a bird-watching book." That was before he learned to give gifts with some get-up-and-go— like Allison's Harley.

You'd never guess Allison was a motorcycle mama. She lives in a suburb where most people prefer Mercedes and BMWs. Allison lives a life of breathtaking gentility. She does volunteer work, plays bridge, and belongs to two country clubs. She also belongs to two other exclusive clubs, both HOGs. HOG stands for Harley Owners Group. "Those are the real bikers," Allison says. "I also ride with what we call RUBs, rich urban bikers. These are biker wanna-bes, doctors and lawyers who ride on the weekend. They carry their portable phones and call themselves the Cells' Angels."

Allison is not your average weekend rider. "I did twenty-five thousand miles on my Harley the first year." She keeps her designer duds for the country club. She rides in fringed and studded biker leather. Biker leather has a harder finish than baby-soft yuppie leather. It's supposed to be armor against a spill on the road. Lord knows what Allison's studded leather bustier protects her against.

How did Allison's golfer husband learn to recognize her biker needs?

"The hard way," she says. "One anniversary, he forgot. He didn't get me anything. He was mortified. I made sure of that. I had a feeling he'd forget, so I bought him a doubly nice gift: a paisley silk dressing gown."

Ooooh. Being nice is the meanest thing a woman can do. If Allison yelled and screamed, Bill could work off his embarrassment in righteous indignation. But when Allison stayed sweet and gave him an extra special gift, she threw another log on the flames of his guilt.

"After that, he made sure his secretary marked down the date," she says.

He still needed a woman to help him remember.

"I mocked him about that. Now he remembers by himself."

Bill's reformation has been amazing. "One year he got me a Mercedes, the little sporty one, black with gold trim. That was a wonderful shocking surprise. For our eighteenth anniversary, he gave me a gorgeous diamond ring."

Allison is not ashamed to drop hints. She thinks it's important to help her man. She doesn't plink a few small thought-pebbles at him, either. Her hints land on the guy like a cast-iron safe falling out a six-story window.

Take the anniversary Harley. Allison saw it first. "It reminded me of when we were first married. Bill and I had trail bikes. We had so much fun riding them." Then their two kids came along, and Allison and Bill became responsible adults.

"My youngest is twenty now. When he left home, I said, 'I've worried about the kids for twenty-three years. Now it's time for them to worry about me.' I saw this wonderful bike, but it wasn't for sale. I called all over and finally found one just like it, miles away at another Harley shop. I told Bill that's what I wanted for our anniversary. He said, 'I bought you a wonderful piece of jewelry.'

"I said, 'No, I want the bike. But what was the jewelry?'

" 'You don't want to know,' said Bill.

"He probably had the last laugh when it came to the cost.

But I love that Harley. It's a Springer soft-tail 1340cc loaded with chrome-and-gold trim. You call that extra trim 'eagle iron,' and you never get finished with it. I had to go out and get every piece of chrome and hang myself in leather. My bike even has leather saddlebags and an eagle on the fender with eyes that light up."

The point isn't that Allison had to ask for her Harley. The point is Bill gave it to her. "I could have bought that bike myself, but it's not the same."

Allison also works to change the next generation. "I've tried to teach my son that it's important to remember birthdays and anniversaries. I hope someday his wife will thank me."

A husband doesn't have to compete with Donald Trump and Richard Burton to give a woman a memorable present. Sometimes, a man has to have more courage than money. But it can be worth the risk. Cindy Lane still remembers her best anniversary present, years later.

"We went to dinner at the Cheshire Inn. After dinner, I thought we were walking back to the car, but instead, he put a key into one of the fantasy room suites and it opened. On the coffee table were three presents to open from Victoria's Secret. Needless to say, *that* night is still in my memory bank . . . verrrry good . . . "

So good, she won't reveal what went on behind those closed doors. Or which fantasy suite it was: the Roman bathhouse, the oriental luxury of the Raj, or the Safari Rainforest. But a man who takes a woman into a fantasy suite is not there to watch David Letterman.

That present wouldn't buy the front bumper on a Mercedes, but it sure made Cindy happy. "Umm, now pricey is not necessarily better," Cindy says. "I think one rose is as good as a dozen. Jewelry always works. But jewelry is one time when you do not go cheap. Zircons will never, ever cut it, ya know?"

Susan B. knows. Some women try to ignore their husband's shopping impairment. They are so happy to get anything for their anniversary, they try to overlook the actual gift. Consider the sad case of Susan. She is a teacher who fell in love with another teacher. John had one son, Jason, and a lot of debts.

"When we were first dating, John was absolutely broke," Susan says. "For our first real date, he took me to a Cardinals baseball game. I didn't care about the Cardinals, but I did care about John. On our first anniversary, I saw two Cardinals tickets on the mantle. I was thrilled that John had remembered. I was not thrilled with his choice of a baseball game, but there was so much sentimental value, because of our first date.

"Then my stepson, Jason, called to ask what time Dad was picking him up for the game.

"On the next anniversary, John formally invited me to dinner and a Cards game. The tickets were free for subscribing to the cable channel, but it was the thought. When we got to the stadium, he discovered the tickets were for the previous night."

Susan chose to overlook these unsuitable gifts. She regretted it a few years later. "Some teenagers broke into our house and ripped off a bunch of our stuff. They took our ten-year-old's piggy bank, a tape player, and some of my jewelry. These boys had been to several houses, and the police recovered some of their loot. My husband and I had to go to the station and identify it. The police would pull out things and I would say, 'Yes, yes, that's mine.' Then the police pulled out a zircon necklace. I said, 'No. I don't wear tacky jewelry like that.' John said, 'Yes, you do. I gave that to you two Christmases ago.'"

He did, too. Susan had buried the necklace in her jewelry

box and forgotten it. "The police wouldn't give it to us because we argued over it."

John's gift giving has gotten better in the nineteen years they've been married. "He won't let me give him hints," Susan says. "He takes his chances. Most often he watches when he is stuck shopping with me. If I say I like something, he sneaks back and buys it."

Sometimes he is simply inspired. "On my fortieth birthday, John surprised me with plans to visit friends in England. That was one of my best gifts ever, even though he admitted to all that it was out of desperation. The other best birthday was a hot-air balloon ride. I'd always wanted one."

Susan was touched. She knew John hated heights. But he was willing to take her anywhere she desired, even into the wild blue yonder. After the flight, John had another reason to dislike heights. "We crash landed," Susan says, still delighted as only a second-grade teacher can be. "It was a fantastic gift."

Some men use a hit-or-miss approach with their gift-giving. Other men recognize that they have a problem and systematically work to correct it. I'm proud to present Tom Finan. He cured himself of a serious shopping disability. It wasn't easy. In fact, the cure took years. But he did succeed. Here is Tom's story in his own words.

"On our first anniversary I came into the bedroom and sat on the end of the bed. During that year my father and grandmother died, my maternal grandfather had a stroke, and my sisters Teri and Peggy had each wrecked my Mom's car—Teri twice.

" 'Well, it's been a great year,' I bubbled to my wife Barb.

"Barb gaped at me in disbelief, blurting '*it has not*,' before bursting into tears.

"On our second anniversary I wished to atone and made a dinner reservation and bought theater seats."

Unfortunately, Tom also ate raw onions with his lunch. "Late in the afternoon I was stricken with the diverticulitis-like pain that raw onions sometimes brought on. About six P.M. I padded down the stairs in my Jockey shorts and sat on the bottom step. 'I really do feel well enough to go to the theater now,' I said between gritted teeth. Barb raised an eyebrow and pointed back up the stairs.

"On our third anniversary, I invited my best friend to join us with his girlfriend for dinner. They were also bringing my really romantic present for Barb: a fancy, and expensive, electric coffee grinder. They showed up four hours late.

"Amazingly, Barb did not feel that a coffee grinder was an appropriate expression of love and affection. At least she didn't attempt to put it to innovative new uses. Later the two of us returned the grinder and bought a little Norfolk pine, which she loved and we used as our Christmas tree that year."

Tom had developed a real knack for buying the wrong gift. "I bought enough expensive custom jewelry to open a Tiffany's outlet—for a woman who dresses in jeans and purchased seven pairs of shoes in twenty years of marriage."

Somewhere along the line Tom noticed that although he liked expensive clothes, gadgets, and jewelry, Barb did not. She preferred simple things. Which may be why she married Tom. He studied his wife's ways and learned to give her the small, personal presents she loved.

"There are always cards and notes, tiny little presents that appeal to her hobbies and whims (okay, maybe sometimes the occasional discreet inlaid gold pin with semiprecious stones) and dinner at one of her favorite informal restaurants with spring flowers on the table. It may not have been a great first year, but it certainly has gotten better."

Tom is a self-made man: He became a thoughtful giver.

Other men naturally have the gift of giving. Jinny says her husband Jim Peterson has completely satisfied her for forty years for every holiday. Jim is quite modest about his achievement. He told Jinny, "Many people give things that they would like to receive themselves instead of focusing on the recipient."

Jinny is happy to take the credit for Jim. She thinks it helps that they married young. "I raised him from a pup, don't forget. He couldn't vote or buy liquor when we married, and he had to have his mom's permission to marry. She paid for the marriage license, too."

Jim's gifts are ingenious. When they had three young children and one station wagon, which he had to take to work, he managed to get Jinny a set of wheels. This was in the early sixties, now, when most women stayed home with the kids. "For Mother's Day, 1963, Jim gave me a red Schwinn with a wicker basket and three gears. I used to put my tiny Lisa on the handlebars with her feet in the basket and off we would wheel. I just loved it. I never had a nice bike growing up, just an old wreck with rubber hand grips that made your hands black. Nobody gave grownups bikes back then, except Jim. Later everyone got a bike, but I was a neighborhood sensation at the time.

"Flash forward to 1964. I started college. For Christmas Jim gave me a Smith-Corona portable typewriter, bright orange." Once again, Jinny was ahead of her time. Well-bred wives did not go back to college. They took care of their children. If they were bored, they drank white wine in the afternoon, went shopping, or did charity work. One neighbor even called Jinny a hippie when she went back to school, and that was not a compliment. But Jim took Jinny—and her goals—seriously. That's why the orange typewriter meant so much to her.

"It was such a vote of confidence that I would need it in

college. A total surprise, too. I still have it here in the office. Our kids took it to college. It is indestructible."

So is Jim's belief in Jinny. He continues to delight her with concert tickets on her birthday and a silly heart-shaped kite for Valentine's Day. When he took business trips to Denmark, he scoured the antique shops for the blue enamelware she craved.

"We wait with bated breath for what he thinks up next. All this *and* he has kept his figger and his hair. A paragon."

If Jim Peterson is a paragon for his perfection, Ed Pieper is a dream for his delightful fault. "Ed gives wonderful things," says Beverly Pieper. "He gave me a red LeBaron convertible for our twelfth anniversary."

Who wouldn't like that present? But Beverly also treasures the poem Ed wrote the year before that and had framed for her. "I have it in our bedroom," she says with pride. You might think the verses are a little corny, but she loves every word. The poem begins, "As we conclude our eleventh year, I feel compelled to say thank you, my dear . . ."

If Beverly is happy with these presents, what's Ed's problem?

"Let me tell you what happened when we were in Italy with another couple, John and Susie," she says. "I have a frog collection, with somewhere over four hundred frogs. Susie pointed out this great frog in this little shop. Ed made a big deal out of getting me away so Susie could buy it and I wouldn't know it. He was going to give it to me for Christmas. He was so excited. The next day I saw Susie and said to her, 'Oh, Ed got me the cutest frog.' "

The charade in the shop was for nothing. Ed's secret didn't even last one night.

You can see why Ed's fault is so much fun. There's no waiting. "He's incredibly generous. He constantly gives. I'll get three and four presents before each holiday and anniversary because he can't keep them a secret. Then he'll buy me one to open on that day, too."

If a man has to have a problem, showering you with presents sounds like a good one. No wonder this couple has survived eighteen years of marriage. It could be that Ed's gift giving is related to another talent many men rarely have: He loves to shop.

Some women feel they don't have to give a man a gift for Valentine's Day or their anniversary. Or they give a perfunctory present—white shirts or dark socks. Beverly puts some thought into her gifts to Ed.

"Ed always says about our marriage, 'We'll give it a shot for the first hundred years and see how it goes.'

"For our fifth anniversary, I bought him a new wedding band with five diamonds. We went to dinner at a restaurant. I arranged for the waitress to bring it to the table in a champagne glass. Ed said to the waitress, 'I think you dropped your ring in my glass.' She said, 'It's not my ring.' Inside I'd engraved, 'Five down, ninety-five to go.' "

Ed, Tom, and Jim are all over forty. They have had time to become wise in the ways of monogamy. But there is hope for the younger generation, too. Sue is so proud of Jeff's gifts. She appreciates what he goes through each time he buys her something. And yet, he is new to monogamy. Jeff is thirty-one. Sue is thirty.

"Jeff likes giving gifts, but he hates shopping for them," Sue says. "In fact, he hates shopping, period. He has a hard time making a decision. He looks and looks and finally buys something. But he's never totally sure that his decision was correct, even after you say you love it. He'll be like, 'Well, I saw this other thing that I thought you'd like, but I decided on this.' He's kinda goofy that way.

"I've liked all the presents he's bought me. Sometimes I

think what he buys for me is really for both of us, but lots of people do that. Like a couple years ago, we both wanted the *Beauty and the Beast* video, so he bought it for me."

Jeff also finds things with special meaning, just for Sue. He charmed her with a childhood favorite, the complete works of *Winnie the Pooh,* with the original drawings. And he doesn't let his fear of buying stop him.

"Jeff has never forgotten Valentine's Day. We always make each other Zoo Parents and help support an animal at the St. Louis Zoo each year. It's kind of a tradition now. We've been doing it for five years. I think it's a good present. Doesn't clutter up the house, and the money goes to a good cause. Next year, I think he's going to adopt the flying fox for me. She has the sweetest face. We can sit and watch her for a long time.

"As for an anniversary, we actually don't have one. We're not sure when exactly we started going out. We started out as friends, and it just evolved into a relationship. Neither one of us remembers exactly when it happened. We'll have anniversaries when we get married. It's no big deal. . . ."

Ah, if only that were true.

CHAPTER 6
Close Shaves

Monogamy takes two. Men are often bashed for missing anniversaries and other monogamous mortal sins. But women deserve a few whacks, too.

I am sorry to say that women can be as insensitive as any beer-bellied Bubba. We're just harder to catch at it. Again and again, we fail to recognize the issues that are important to men.

I discovered this at age fifteen. I learned the hard way. My failure to understand what a razor means to a man was the closest shave I ever had. I was baby-sitting at home. I'd packed the kids off to bed and settled in for a nice three-hour talk on the phone with my best friend Sue. In the days before call-waiting, this was a risky business.

I didn't know my father had been trying to call home for two and a half hours.

He didn't know I was using his razor to shave my legs.

It was a nasty shock when he stormed through the kitchen door and caught me. There I was talking on the phone, wearing shorts and a baggy sweatshirt. I was sitting on the Formica counter with my soaped-up legs in the kitchen sink. I was shaving them with Dad's Gillette razor.

He was speechless. At least in the beginning. I was lucky to escape alive.

That's when I first learned that men freak out when women use their razors. Even worse, men can't explain why they don't like it. Ask the smartest man you know why a woman shouldn't use his razor, and you'll get one of these dumb answers:

- It dulls the blade
- It rearranges the molecules
- Women don't do it right
- It's too personal

That last remark comes from a man who'll let selected women share his life and his toothbrush. But no one gets her hands on his razor.

We women can't understand this. We figure if he can run his hands along our thighs, we can run his razor there, too. We resent the fact that there is one thing he won't share. We can't understand, and he can't explain.

A shrink who won't let his wife use his razor says, "Some things are men's things."

What kind of answer is that?

"You want a rational explanation for the irrational," he says.

A man with the Gillette Company in Boston has another explanation. "A woman shaves a greater area. If you took the square feet of her legs—if I can say that—you'd see there's much more shaving area. It's the equivalent of two or three blade shaves. The blade gets much more damage. A man's face is so sensitive he knows just how many shaves are left on his blade. The razor is so personal, it becomes part of him. When his pattern is interrupted, it throws him off. That's why men don't like to share their razors."

After years of condemning men for being insensitive, we

find one area where they're quivering exquisitely. And we dismiss it out of hand. Women refuse to understand why men don't just pop in a fresh blade and shut up.

Dwayne, a full-time shaver, had the most rational irrational argument.

"There's an easy explanation," he says. "You know how poets rhapsodize about a woman's raven hair, but if they find one strand in the butter, they go crazy? Well, many men like women with smooth legs. But heaven help them if the women use the guys' razor. Women think we'll never know if they clean it up and put it back in the cabinet. But we do. We're not that dumb.

"See, shaving is one of the most basic rituals of manhood. Here's how it works: It's morning, and you stumble in. You look in the mirror and make a few faces. You lather up. You start to shave. It's a wonderful feeling.

"But if a woman has used your razor, things happen you'll never believe," Dwayne says. "You draw that blade down your cheek, and it's as if the flesh is coming off your skull. The pain is immediate. You can feel your teeth coming through your cheek. You feel like every whisker has been torn out by hand.

"It's happened to us all at least once. After that, we never trust women again. At least, not with razors."

For successful monogamy, we women need to sharpen our sensitivity. We need to respect the privacy of a man's razor. We also need to recognize another sore spot. We must understand a man's obsession with his hair.

I knew men had a strange thing about their hair. I didn't know how strange until I spent a day with Ron Popeil. Ron is the TV pitchman who used to peddle the Veg-O-Matic on late-night TV. He went from slicing and dicing to spraying. He sold spray-on hair in a can. At the time, I was working for a St. Louis TV station. Popeil said he'd fly in from Los Angeles to spray a head in the heartland.

My demonstration model was Bob Levine. In the seventies, Bob was a wily university radical. Now he is a suburban papa who enjoys coaching his daughter's softball team. There was just one small spot of discontent in Bob's life. It was on his head. Bob's thick black hair was receding. To cover his bald spot, he let pitchman Popeil spray his head in public. I thought this was an experiment in spot salesmanship. That's not how the guys who gathered to watch the demonstration saw it. Popeil gave hope to his fellow man.

I could see it in their faces. They looked like plane crash survivors when the rescuers parachute in. Saved! They were going to be saved.

Popeil covered Bob's bald spot with something that looked like hair from twenty feet. Up close, Bob's head resembled a grocery store coconut.

It was pathetic. It was more pathetic when Bob's hair sweated off that same night. Worse, it happened while Bob was coaching his daughter's softball team. Black streaks starting running down his forehead. The nine-year-old girls on the team screamed. Bob reached for his pocket handkerchief and wiped off his spray-on hair. His dream died.

Even then, some men wanted to believe. They would take me aside and say, "It would work for me, wouldn't it? I'm not as bald as he is."

Sure. As long as you live like a potato in a cool, dry place. In the St. Louis heat and humidity, I'd say you could have hair about six days a year.

I tried to be kind. But I wanted to laugh at these guys, the way they laughed at us. It's different for women. We divide our anxieties. We worry about our figures, our thighs, and the crow's feet around our eyes. Men have one main worry:

their hair. That's why it's so powerful. They have only one way to torment themselves.

And they do.

Want to drive a man crazy? Say this, "Are you getting a little thin on top, Clyde, or is that a trick of the light?" Clyde will spend hours examining his hair, convinced it's eroding like a California beach.

"When you're young," a man told me, "you get up in the morning and look for coffee. When you're middle-aged, you get up and look for your hair on the pillow. When you're old, you don't bother. You know it's gone."

That's what this male hair fetish is about—getting old. Women go through menopause. But it's not so public or capricious. We know roughly when it will happen. A guy can go bald at twenty. At forty. At seventy. Then Nature, that mean mother, turns around and gives him hair where he doesn't want it—in his ears and nose. But sometimes, for no reason, she'll let a man keep it all. That hair won't give him happiness. Until the day he dies, he'll worry about losing it.

Sensitive women need to understand this bald truth to survive monogamy: For men, true nakedness is an uncovered head.

They may parade around the locker room without a stitch. But let their carefully draped strands shift and show their bald spots, and the same men will log more mirror time than teenagers, putting their hair right.

You'd think men would have compassion for their fellow men who are losing it. No. Some ugly herd instinct takes over. Men giggle at drape heads. They cackle when a gust of wind makes some poor TV guy's sprayed and draped hair flop up like a pot lid. They point out to women, who don't care, which men are wearing bad toupees. They make fun of guys with receding hairlines who compensate with ponytails. If you say a guy's ponytail looks sexy, nine out of ten men will snarl: "Looks like he yanked his hair backwards."

Men are bitchier than women could ever be.

When men see the Popeil demonstration on TV, they'll tell some bald guy, "Hey, Bill, you should try that stuff." I was aghast the first time I heard a pack of men turn on one of their balding friends this way. If I saw a diet commercial, I'd never walk up to a fat woman and say, "Hey, Tubbo, you should try that."

I might think it, but I wouldn't say it.

Maybe that's why the ultimate male insult is to call a man bald. If men don't like their boss, they won't call him a crook. They admire crooks. They won't even call him a wimp. He's "the bald bastard." They add the bastard to take the edge off the insult. If they really hate the guy, they call him Baldy.

Women cannot understand the depth of this insult. It's like calling someone a "cad" in Victorian England. It means nothing to us. Women think some bald men are sexy. Look at Sean Connery. At the very least, if we like the guy, we don't care if he's losing his hair.

Try telling that to a man. He won't believe you. As my friend tried to explain: "A man's Achilles heel is on his head."

That image made my eyes cross. But I knew what he meant.

Monogamy is becoming more equal. Men aren't just helping with the household chores. They're starting to share the pain. Women like to believe we are the only sex who suffers. To stay young and attractive, women will lift their face and fanny, dye their hair, wax their lips and legs, and whine: "Would men go through this for us? They expect us to look good while they get old and don't care."

Woman, you are wrong. Men are beginning to suffer for the pursuit of youth. They just don't talk about it. Once again, the sensitive area is that male soft spot, his head. I mean, the hair on his head. Sadly, most men do the arcane practice I'm about to describe to please their wives. They, too, know it hurts to maintain monogamy.

I'm about to let you in a manly beauty secret: body hair tinting. As a body gets older, the hair turns gray from head to toe. Women can dye some and shave the rest. Men didn't used to be so lucky. But now a few silver foxes have the brass to change their graying bodies.

These men have given makeup artist Giac Ghianni of Ghianni Aesthetics a colorful sideline. Giac does not have some slick salon in Manhattan. He works in the heart of the heartland: Cape Girardeau and Kansas City, Missouri. These are cities where the rest of the country imagines men wear CAT hats and chew tobacco. They are the last places where you'd expect straight men to go to Giac for something faintly kinky: Giac tints their body hair.

It began when a woman customer said her husband was a new man. From the neck up. "She said he had a new hairpiece," Giac says. "She said her husband looked years younger."

The piece gave the man the darker, fuller hair of his youth. Alas, a hairpiece can only cover so much. "Once the clothes came off, his chest and legs were gray." The illusion of youth was gone. Gray reality took root.

"I told her hair can be tinted. Actors do it all the time."

Giac offered to show her husband how to tint his body hair. "It's an easy process. Any man can learn it in one lesson. It worked for him. Word got around. In one month, I did eighteen body tintings for men. They all either have hairpieces or tint the hair on their head."

These are the last men you'd expect to dye. "Most of these guys are very outdoorsy. When their shirts are unbuttoned, they want their chest hair to match their heads." Others want their collars and cuffs to match in the locker room or swimming pool.

I had to ask: If a guy dyes, does he get roots on his arms and legs?

"No. Body hair comes in gradually. If you tint once a month, no one will notice. If you get lazy and wait three months, everyone will know when you go from gray to brown."

Color him lightly, boys. You don't want to fade to black. At twenty, your hair may have been raven. But at sixty, you're safer making it light or medium brown. Those fish-belly legs will look out of season with new black hair.

Giac charges forty-five dollars for a chest and arm lesson. A full body tint is $100. But he'll tell you how to do it for free. "You can buy several good hair tints for men at the supermarket or the drugstore. You leave the tint on five or ten minutes, then rinse it off in the shower. That's it."

Almost. Giac adds this chilling reminder. "When you rinse off the tint, use cool water. Hot water opens the pores, and they will grab color. That could leave your skin dyed dark for days." Instead of showing off your hairy young chest, you'll be stuck in the last refuge of the crepe drape, turtlenecks.

Giac recommends something suitable when you're giving yourself a full-body tint. "Wear an old Speedo swimsuit. That way you can see to cover the whole area. If you do it right, it looks like a tan line."

One more thing: "You have to stand around with this tint on for a while. Be careful. Don't brush up against the wallpaper. Don't sit down on your wife's favorite chair. You'll tint it, too. I had one man who did that. He sat down on the bedspread and ruined it."

It didn't look youthful. But the blast from his wife took years off his life.

This is another example of women's insensitivity to man. There he is, dyeing to please her, and she yells at him for ruining a bedspread.

I've shown that women do not understand the skin-deep issue of razors and baldness. But most of all, women do not appreciate how delicate men are when it comes to sex. Men are romantic creatures, who are easily turned off by women's coarse, direct approach. Especially when it comes to group sex.

The story of Ray the Cab Driver is a typical male reaction to female forays on the edge of monogamy. When respectable women lust in our hearts, nice men are shocked. And Ray is nice. He's a churchgoer with one child. He's a big man, with skin the color of coffee beans. He has breakfast most mornings in a city diner. One morning, his dark, shiny skin was tinged with gray. It was obvious he'd had a bad night driving his cab. Ray told me about it.

"So I'm driving across the Poplar Street Bridge late at night when this woman throws her underwear over my head," he says.

Ray is a tolerant man. After all, she was a paying customer.

"It was okay, as long as it didn't interfere with my driving. But when she started waving her lingerie out the window at that truck driver, I drew the line. That's dangerous."

All it takes is one little slip.

"I hate ladies' night. And this was the worst—ladies' night at Oz, the Illinois club."

Sometimes, women are not only equal—they're better. When it comes to crude carousing, Ray takes his hat off to women. But that's all he takes off, no matter what they ask him.

Four women on a night out can make a hotel full of male conventioneers look like a temperance meeting, Ray says. We're faster, too. Women can pack a weekend of revelry into one night. "But they don't do this alone. Women have to go in groups because they need to encourage each other. These are not wild women. They are the pillars of the community. I'm talking about Mrs. Accountant, Mrs. Lawyer, Mrs. Judge, Mrs. Homemaker. But get them together, and they get a wonderful sense of courage and bravery. That latent bit of rowdyism that sleeps in us all is awakened. They get a little crazy. Just for one night, once in a while.

"I picked up my four women at Oz after they'd been watching the male dancers. They started out the ride verbally beating up their husbands for being wimps. They made a couple of frisky remarks to me, but I didn't take them too seriously. When we got on the Poplar Street Bridge, one of them spotted a truck driver in the next lane. She rolled down the window and tried to talk to him. But he didn't pay much attention."

Ray didn't, either. "That's when another woman put her underwear on my head. Then she decided talking to the truck driver wouldn't get his attention, so she started waving her underwear out the window. The truck driver loved it. He was blasting his horn.

"Those ladies asked me the wildest questions. They were so personal, I couldn't answer them. I felt sorry for their husbands when they got home."

Why?

"Let's say these women were full of the lust for life."

Then the guys should be happy.

"A poor husband doesn't have a chance. He's never going to be the man she saw dancing that night."

Ray sees these women as part of a trend. "In the sixties, men used to go to the Playboy Club and watch those young women in those little costumes. At first, I thought the women weren't too bright. But then I saw the tips they were taking in. Most of them were tucking in those tips and laughing at us fool men. Now I figure it's the men's turn. Most of those male dancers are sticking dollar bills in their shorts and laughing at those fool women."

I watched the seminaked guys dance once and never went back. I felt like one of those fat old guys who smokes cigars and leers. I wanted the men to put some clothes on and talk to me. I must be getting old.

"That's not old," Ray says. "When you want them to put on their clothes and go away, then you're old."

What Ray can't understand is that these women are faithful. If he'd actually pulled over so they could meet the trucker, they'd probably clam up and act like the PTA meeting was called to order. They felt safe waving their underwear out the window because they knew a man like Ray would never do anything risky.

These women were simply indulging in the female sport of lusting in their hearts. Men don't understand that many women use group lust to stay monogamous. They get release from the pressures of monogamy in public, in the company of other married women. Then they go back home and stand by their man for the next year. It's the modern version of the chaperone.

There's no better illustration of this than the night the male dancers came to the Elks Club. Janice Bequette Jones was there. From her account, I believe the Elks made the mistake many married men make: They thought so-called nice women wouldn't—no, couldn't—act this way. The evening, Janice says, was a revelation. Maybe not for the

Elks women. They didn't see anything they hadn't seen before.

But the Elks men were reeling. They saw their wives, mothers, and grandmothers screaming, "Bring on the men!" The same wives, mothers, and grandmothers who worked so tirelessly for the club barbecues and Christmas baskets.

They were tireless that night, too. "The three hundred screaming women got out of hand," Janice says. Here's what she says happened:

"My town is a bump in the road with one tavern and two clubs, the VFW and the Elks. Some of the Elkettes got the idea to have male dancers at the Elks club. It was a first for us."

The male Elks thought it was cute to let the "girls" have a good time. Besides, the proceeds would go to the club.

"My town has fewer than two thousand people. Three hundred women showed up for the dancers. It was the biggest attendance for any Elks event. Even bigger than the New Year's Eve dance."

All those . . . er, expectant women—and now there was no show. "One stripper got lost and couldn't find the place. That delayed the show forty minutes. They kept playing this loud music: BOOM, BOOM, BOOMP! I think it got everyone stirred up."

At last, the male stripper found the town. The show was on. Or off.

"There weren't enough strippers to go around, so the younger and leaner Elks were waiters." Topless waiters. The Elks wore black pants, collars, and cuffs. They were the same guys who hung around the club bar, but the women looked at them with new respect.

"I didn't recognize them with their shirts off," Janice says. "By the end of the evening, some Elk waiters were dancing on the tables. I think they made more money than the dancers. At my table were some wild women who came in a limo. They 'pantsed' the waiter—pulled his pants off. Fortunately, he came prepared and wore black bikini underwear. Another Elk waiter had a table of very old women. They didn't tip much, but they pinched him a lot.

"Even the wife of the Exalted Ruler seemed to be having a good time.

"A large woman got rather carried away and was removed, but not before she pulled a scissors out of her purse and cut a dancer's G-string. She yelled, 'I'll be back.'

"I could not bring myself to put any money in our dancer's G-string," Janice says. "I think it was my 1950s Catholic upbringing. Sister Mary Rose told me never to put money in men's pants."

But all the women put money into the Elks' hands. "It was the biggest moneymaker the club had in a long time. Now some men are hollering they want their turn. But others say no."

Why not?

"Everyone says women strippers for men are different. In a way, they're right. Men don't think like us. I didn't come out of there turned on. I was laughing my head off."

Janice says male dancers aren't really about sex. They're about sexual revenge. They're how women get back for being treated like men's toys.

"We've had to put up with men looking at us that way. Now we can take out our frustrations on them. Let the guys know what it's like. I don't think men's night would be like that. I also don't think the men would let their wives watch them make fools of themselves, like we did."

It is important that women, who demand men be more sensitive, stay sensitive to men's feelings. Especially young

men, with long blond hair, good bodies, and hard muscles.
Like those nice male dancers. I'm pleased to say that based
on my observation, the experience is mutually satisfying.
Both the women and the male dancers get something.

To promote such understanding, I once spent a night in
the male dancers' dressing room. It was embarrassing for a
happily married woman like me to have to watch those
handsome young men run around with practically nothing
on, oiling their firm, naked chests, combing their long hair,
pulsing their perky pecs. But I did it for women everywhere.

Those men were nearly naked, but they weren't ashamed
to share. They used my hair spray. I used their confidences.
I learned how they suffered for their art. They made a couple of hundred dollars a night in tips for gyrating in a break-
away costume, but it wasn't easy money.

One came back to the dressing room, sweating and
loaded with dollar bills stuck in amazing places. He
dumped a G-string load in a cardboard box the size of a
microwave oven. He confided that the biggest women gave
the biggest bills. "The bigger they are, the more they tip.
About 250 pounds. Those are my favorites."

He had deep red scratches on his belly and below from
the women's long nails when they put their bills in his G-
string.

I saw that sensitivity cuts both ways.

CHAPTER 7
In the Ring: How to Fight Like a Married Person

We had our first fight on our honeymoon.

The quarrel started because we had too much of everything: too much sex, too much champagne, and too much of each other.

We were staying at the Plaza Hotel in New York. This was the fourth day of the honeymoon, and we hadn't been out of the room for more than a few hours.

The night before, I'd polished off a bottle of champagne mixed with four bottles of Guinness stout. Don called this mixture Black Velvets. They went down smooth and wicked.

They woke me up, mean and nasty. It was now two in the morning. I didn't feel like I'd been drinking Black Velvets. I felt like I'd been eating old carpets. My stomach heaved and churned like the storm-tossed North Atlantic. A gale of acid indigestion was going on down there. Ugh. Urp. Yecch.

I crawled into the bathroom and lay down on the cool white tile floor. The hotel housekeeper would probably find me here in the morning, dead. I hoped so. I couldn't live like this. I just wanted to throw up and die.

Don poked his head into the bathroom and said, "Are you all right?"

"Uhhh," I groaned, like something from a freshly opened tomb.

"Reuben's deli is open all night," he said. "Can I get you something to soothe your stomach?"

It wasn't fair. The man drank even more than I did, and he looked like he'd spent the night swilling soda water. That irritated me, but I summoned the strength for a deathbed request:

"Just a little white meat of turkey," I said. "On a slice of white bread."

I put my head on the rim of the cool white toilet and fell asleep.

Next thing I knew, Don was back with a disgusting, smelly, paper-wrapped mound. He had an innocent, proud look, like a retriever that's just brought a dead rabbit into the drawing room.

In this case, it was a dead turkey. Almost a full pound of it, covered with mounds of pickles, onions, and sour cream, all of it swimming on a raft of Russian rye. My stomach flopped like a freshly caught trout.

"You beast!" I screamed. "How could you do this to me?"

"You said you wanted turkey," he said, looking puzzled.

I shut the sandwich in the bathroom. The smell was so strong it broke down the door and invaded the whole room. While I lay there, dying, Don not only ate his pastrami, he also ate that monstrous turkey, onion, and sour cream, and looked even happier.

The next morning, I ate soda crackers and brooded. Five days into this marriage, and I'd made a mistake. A man who would bring a sandwich like that to a dying woman was too insensitive to be married.

I didn't need him. I didn't need any man. I could have a good time in New York on my own.

"I'm leaving," I announced and slammed the door. Let him figure out if it was for the evening or forever.

There was a French movie house near the hotel. I didn't know what the French movie was because I didn't know any French, but I'd go anyway and get some culture. I was a sophisticated married woman of twenty-one. I bought my ticket, stomped into the theater, and took a seat. Funny. The audience was all men — single men sitting alone. One sat down next to me. He had a newspaper over his lap, and he was making grunting noises. So were the people on the screen.

It was a French movie all right. That was one of the things they were doing on screen, along with a lot of other odd lickings and strokings. I was in a French porn movie, but not for long. I left, too embarrassed to get my money back.

When I came back to our room, we went to a soothing dinner at a French restaurant, which was a lot better than a French movie. I decided I would try to work out this marriage.

I had a lot to learn about monogamous fighting. Instead of flouncing out like a spoiled child, I could have handled our differences in an open and adult manner.

When people say that monogamy is dull, they don't realize how they can liven it up with a good fight. A monogamous squabble is not a simple sharing of insults. You must stretch your memory and your vocabulary. For instance, I could have turned our little contretemps into a critique of his family and friends, as in this sample argument between a newly married couple.

SHE: You beast! How could you do this to me? I've done nothing but suffer since I met you. It's bad enough I had to put up with your best man for four days before the wedding.

HE: Bill was my best friend in the Army. He said if I ever needed someone to stand up for me, he'd be there.

SHE: If you paid him.

HE: Bill needed a little help. He was embarrassed to ask me for money.

SHE: Is that why he gave you an itemized bill for his plane ticket and travel expenses, including the cab fare to the airport, a two-dollar charge for bottled water and a voucher for his lost wages?

HE: If we're talking about money, what about your brother Zeke, who tried to hit me up for a loan for his alternative farming project?

SHE: I think it's wonderful that Zeke wants to start his own business.

HE: I don't think growing pot is legal.

Note how he cleverly changed the subject from his best friend to her worst brother. It's much more fun to argue with someone you know instead of some stranger. You don't know a stranger's psychic sore spots. When you and your beloved live together a little longer, your fights will get even more interesting. After all, you alone know his secret hurts. Maybe he was passed over for promotion. The position he wanted went to his bitter rival. He did such a good job of pretending that everyone else believes he didn't want to make the move. When you argue, you can remind him of the truth:

"No wonder you were passed over for promotion," you may say. "You can't even remember to take out the trash, much less run the entire Omaha office."

Don't forget he, too, knows your vulnerable spots:

"Oh, yeah, well if I was going to get anywhere, it would be no thanks to you. You're just like your mother. You even look like her."

Zing. This is your worst nightmare. In fact, just the other morning he saw you looking at your fishbelly legs in the mirror and saying, "Gack. I'm old. I have my mother's rubbery white legs with the blue veins."

A monogamous fight can be a wide-ranging exercise. It includes history: "You never used to forget our anniversary. . . . You always cut down my family. . . . Yours isn't the Brady Bunch, either. I remember the time your mother . . ."

Genealogy: "Hah! I'm not surprised you're hungover this morning. You were with your brother last night, and that's a signal to bring on the booze. Has been as far back as anyone can remember. Your family has enough drunks to start its own AA chapter."

And psychology: "You're driving me nuts."

Some long-married couples try to make fighting more sporting by imposing rules. Cindy Lane and her husband Joe have been married since January 13, 1976. Cindy says, "Life isn't fair, so why should fighting be? Here are some tricks of the trade.

"Regarding in-laws/outlaws: If you are the blood relative, you can call your sister, your mom, or your irritating Aunt Ethel fat, ugly, and stupid. Then, and only then, can your spouse agree. But only the blood relative can start the trashing.

"Regarding kids: The Lane Law states, 'Whoever is around at the time, handles it.' We do not do the 'wait till your father comes home!' routine.

"Regarding money: Give it up. I mean the argument. If you're a chronic overspender, just nod up and down. Vow to change your ways, smile, and do your best. It also helps to go back and figure out how your partner was raised about money. In this case, Joe's mom and dad were frugal and smart. My parents always gave me whatever I asked for whenever I asked for it.

"I thought money was endless, and it was, until the day of my wedding. Boom! Then, before I knew it, I was out there applying for food stamps and paying for my last semester of college. Jeez, I hate learning things the hard way!"

For monogamous, unmarried Maria and Millbrook, fighting style is more important than substance. "Millbrook is a controlled WASP," she says. "When we fight, he gets very upset at what he calls my shouting."

When Maria is ready for a run-in, she raises her voice. In the blue collar world she grew up in, this signaled to your partner that it was time for a serious discussion. It took his attention away from such noisy distractions as the TV, the kids, and the guy next door fixing his car engine. It also warned the kids to scatter. To Millbrook, Maria's method is overly contentious. He lets her know he does not approve of raised voices.

"Then I tell Millbrook, 'That's not shouting. THIS IS SHOUTING!' and really start screaming. His idea of fighting is a college debate. He gets this low, controlled voice. He keeps saying, 'Maria, let's discuss it.' I keep telling him, 'I'm not a guest on Letterman. I'm angry.' WASPs never yell. They show anger in other ways."

Like quietly cutting you out of the will.

"I think we're very lucky," Maria says. "We never fight about serious things. Our fights are always entertaining. That's because early on, when our arguments began to be dull and repetitive, Millbrook and I set an important rule: You cannot bring up old fights in new fights."

They have a double-indemnity clause. This couple gives each other the same advantage as any other criminally accused person in America. When an argument ends, it's a complete acquittal. Once Maria and Millbrook finish an argument, "we cannot bring up the subject again. Never. No matter what."

If Maria is chewing out Millbrook for dropping his clothes all over the living room, she cannot bring in last month's brouhaha when he left his shoes in the hallway and she tripped over them in the dark. Even though the two subjects are related (he's a slob), old arguments about "piggitudinal" behavior are banned. She does not drag in old dustups. Instead, she seeks new and better ways to explore his current transgressions. This keeps their fights fresh.

"It's worked," Maria says. "We used to go round and round on the same old subject. Now we have new and original arguments."

Jinny Peterson has been married to Jim for an incredible forty years. "We feel so lucky we still love each other," Jinny says.

What is the secret of their marital happiness?

"Sulking and pouting," Jinny says. "That's how we've survived. The experts say you should talk it out. But I say there's much to be said for not saying anything. If you don't say anything ugly, then you have nothing to apologize for and he has nothing to forgive and forget."

She believes sulking and pouting are not only acceptable, but sexy. "Do you know that *boudoir* means 'a room in which to pout'?" I have no idea if this is true, since I took Spanish in high school. But if I had to do it over again, I'd learn French. It makes everything sound slightly risqué.

Just because Jinny advocates sulking and pouting doesn't mean Jinny and Jim never disagree. "I like to say that we only had one fight, but we had it every Friday night. Jim came from an unsociable family. I came from a family whose motto was, 'Come on over.' I never had to worry about inviting kids to my parents' house. We always had cake and soda and potato chips for an unplanned party. I thought this way of life would continue when we were married. I wanted the world over on Fridays. When the week was done, Jim liked to put on his oldest clothes and work around the house. He didn't want to see anyone. His idea of a good time was to be by himself.

"I didn't realize this before we were married because we were in school and that was a drop-in environment. Our life didn't settle into a grownup routine until Jim got a job. It was only when I had a baby and couldn't go home to mother and didn't want to anyway that I realized what kind of man I'd married."

So how did you handle it? This is a serious difference.

"We worked it out," Jinny says with a shrug. "I developed a busy daytime life, and at night I sulked and pouted."

True sulkers do not retreat into sullen silence. Jinny salted her sulking with snappy (and snappish) answers. "My favorite, which every woman understands, is: 'Don't start being nice to me at ten o'clock.'

"My other saying is, 'Pretend you live here.' I used that one on the kids, really. It means, 'Pick up your wet towels. This isn't a hotel.'

"Jim and I had two other rules. The first one was, 'No threats.' We never use the D word. We never say, 'I'm going to divorce you.' Second, we never criticize each other's relatives. We knew early on we both had family members who were eminently criticizable.

"Jim and I were both the youngest children in our families. We both married on the (incorrect) assumption that each would take care of the other."

It is a rude awakening when you realize your beloved is not going to wait on you. You can't even use your baby-child tricks and look cute and helpless to get your way. Your significant other is doing the same thing. It becomes a real battle. Some couples are locked in power struggles over who should rule the home. Jim and Jinny fought about who would *not* take charge. Their early discussions went something like this:

SHE: You call.

HE: No, you call.

SHE: I thought you called.

HE: I didn't. I was waiting for you to call.

SHE: (pout)

HE: (sulk)

Sulking and pouting go against all modern advice. But they have been an accepted marital aid for centuries. Often the old ways are still worthwhile. For instance, my grandmother was married fifty years. She told me, "Never go to bed when you've been fighting."

It's still good advice. I never go to bed when I'm angry at Don. Sometimes, it's tough for me to stay up all night, but if I pace around the living room I can do it. By three A.M. I've worked up a full-blown grievance. I can remember back to the time he picked me up thirty minutes late on a date.

To fight properly, some long-married couples say you need perspective. You need to understand how your partner feels. My friend Elea Carey said, "Try to see the argument from the other person's viewpoint. That's what my advisors told me. So I did. I thought, 'Oh, this is what it feels like to be a total asshole. What an enriching experience.'"

And I'll never forget this advice from my married friends: "No matter how angry you are, give your partner credit where it's due. Try to find something positive to say."

They were so right. Looking on the bright side can help lighten the bitterest disappointment. Suppose your spouse has been transferred to some place you find unpalatable. You can still find something good to say about it: "Well, I guess we should look on the bright side of this move to Wet

Blanket, Wisconsin. We'll be nine hundred miles from your mother."

It's also important to acknowledge your husband's role in the rearing of your children. You may have given birth to the child, but the paternal parent has also made important contributions. Even in times of crisis, you can acknowledge them, as in this example: "*Your* son wrecked the van."

If he is his father's son, he is also his mother's child. Don't forget to take your share of credit, too: "*My* son got a scholarship."

Along with the old advice, there is new advice. Instead of storming out and sitting in a movie house with sticky seats, I could have found a nice, clean bookstore and consulted those best-selling authors who are happy to help troubled marriages. I wouldn't need hours of painful, expensive counseling, either. I could save my marriage with a seven-dollar paperback.

One popular paperback Polonius is John Gray, Ph.D. He's sold more than four million copies of *Men Are from Mars, Women Are from Venus* by telling you what you want to hear: Your lover is from another planet.

That explains everything. Sometimes, when you're really angry, you think your loved one has two heads.

Gray often describes women as "soft" and feminine creatures who are gifted with feelings and connectedness. Obviously, women like Roseanne Barr and Cincinnati Red head Marge Schott are from yet another planet. Uranus, perhaps.

What I like about Gray is that he makes marital problems sound so simple. In one of his recent books, *Men, Women and Relationships*, Gray writes:

"A woman needs symbols of love. When a man brings a woman flowers, they validate her beauty and femininity as being of great value. Women need to be given flowers on an ongoing basis. To her, flowers are symbols of a man's love. They make his love concrete."

Flowers may indeed help a woman feel special. They may help a guy get laid. They may give her hay fever. She may be one of those women who wishes her man didn't spend forty-five bucks on something that will be dead in four days. Or she may like her love more solid than concrete. She could want it as hard as diamonds. Or maybe she needs to sur-round herself with softness—a nice soft gold necklace around her neck.

But to go back to our honeymoon hostilities . . . if Don had brought me fragrant flowers instead of a smelly sand-wich, I might have nibbled a few rose petals and then fallen back asleep, hugging the toilet contentedly, secure in the knowledge that my beauty and femininity were validated.

If you read some advice authors, our conflict was probably caused by an unspeakable difference. A whole galaxy of wed-ded bliss-makers believes that not only are men and women aliens from different planets, we speak different languages. These are books like *He Says, She Says: Closing the Commu-nication Gap Between the Sexes* by Lillian Glass. For some rea-son, only the advice authors understand what the opposite sex is saying. For $24.95 (hardback) or $6.99 (paperback), they'll be happy to interpret.

John Gray, for instance, explains that "women break down when they go beyond their limit. The actual factor that causes the breakdown can be likened to the straw that broke the camel's back. It is not the weight of the load that causes her to break down, merely one or two straws. If a man can listen to her tell of all the pressures and responsibilities that are weighing her down, and then offer to lighten her load by carrying a few straws, he will help her tremendously."

If I understand Gray right, and I may not, because I really

do believe this man is from another planet, all a guy has to do is listen to you complain and maybe do the dishes and take the kid to soccer practice.

So does he help you out? No way, says Gray. "A man is generally reluctant to help a woman in her exhausted state, because he assumes the way to help is to identify and then do the most difficult tasks. This is not necessary. Moreover, he will resent doing her most difficult tasks. . . ."

You can't blame him. What if her toughest task is being eight months pregnant and still going to the office? Carrying that ungrateful baby in August is not something a guy wants to take over. It could ruin his legs. Not to mention his flat abs.

Gray explains what goes wrong: "When men are confronted with an exhausted woman, they are notorious for giving lectures on how a woman shouldn't do so much. They say things like: 'You take on too much,' 'Relax, you worry too much,' 'All this is not that important,'" and other advice that may hurt female feelings and cause a fight.

About those fights. Did you ever notice how bloodless advice book arguments are? Their people start a scrap with something like, "I can't believe you'd say that." I can't believe you'd say that, either. Maybe these authors are really talking about people from other planets. Or maybe they deal with very genteel people. The fights I've heard (especially the ones coming from apartment 2A) are much more profane.

I believe some advice books repress the normal monogamous ruckus. This can be harmful to a relationship. In my workshops ("Men Are from Hunger, Women Are from Hell, or Vice Versa Depending on Who's Buying This Book"), I help couples return to a more natural style of squabbling. They learn to express their true feelings when they fight. After buying my books and throwing them at each other, couples are soon arguing in a way that helps them break down the barriers to their feelings—not to mention some crockery and a Pella window.

Consider this sample. The husband has been listening to his wife whine for half an hour about how her ungrateful boss had her write the entire report and then put his name on it. Their house looks like it's been ransacked. The laundry basket is overflowing. She has work piled up on two desks, one at the office and one at home.

How does her husband respond when she says she's under pressure? He may start out arguing in that wimpy advice book fashion, but before long, thanks to my workshops, audio tapes, and books, his argument style is enriched and so is my bank account. It takes a little work. But note how much freer and stronger this couple's language becomes as the fight progresses:

HE: You take on too much. That goddamn company doesn't appreciate it. Those lazy assholes in your department sit around and watch you work yourself to death and then take credit for it. No wonder you're worn out.

SHE: If we're talking about sitting around, you can get off your dead ass and help me now.

HE: What am I supposed to do, read your goddamn mind? If you want something done, say so. Don't go around like a martyr. Speak up, for god's sake.

SHE: (Shouting) CAN YOU HEAR ME NOW, YOU IDIOT?? AM I LOUD ENOUGH?? WHY DO I HAVE TO *TELL* YOU WHAT TO DO? YOU CAN SEE THE TRASH NEEDS TO BE TAKEN OUT, THE KITCHEN FLOOR SHOULD BE SWEPT, AND THE LAUNDRY NEEDS TO BE DONE. ASSUME SOME RESPONSI-BILITY!!!!

HE: Yeah, right, yell at me because you are really mad at your boss.

SHE: I am really, truly, mad at you. Now do you have any more advice for me?

HE: Yes. Shut the hell up.

Isn't that a more natural argument style? By learning to express themselves, this couple will both get what they want. He will stomp out of the house for the rest of evening, giving her the peace she craves to finish her many tasks. She will shut the hell up for at least a week. It will be so cold in their bedroom, their air-conditioning bill will drop significantly. This will save them lots of money, which they can spend on more advice books—or a divorce lawyer.

If I didn't want to invest the time and money in a book, I could find a quick two-buck solution: Get a women's magazine. Every month they solve marriage problems with small, sexy numbers: "Five Ways to Fight Fair," "Six Reasons to Argue Agreeably" and "Seven Steps to Reducing Your Fights and Your Flabby Thighs." You never see "243 Ways to Save Your Marriage."

Women's magazines even give their blessing to an occasional brawl by running advice called "The Fight Happy Couples Should Have." These stories make you think, "We're not happy. Maybe we need a good fight." Sort of the way mother used to say you needed a good laxative.

Women's magazines are also one of the last places you will find anyone advocating the use of feminine wiles. The magazines don't call it that, but they do say you can get your way with flattery. This article in *New Woman* magazine is typical. It's called "Where Flattery Gets You: Compliments and Criticism Can Make or Break a Relationship" by Tessa Albert Warschaw, Ph.D.

It says, "Studies show that people who regularly give and receive compliments have more loving partnerships. Compliments nurture, support, and sustain; they make a relationship grow. Criticism, on the other hand, can kill a relationship. It cuts conversation short and pushes the other person away. But criticism does not have to hurt. It, too, can make a relationship grow—if it is done with love and kindness, at the right time and in the right place."

You can give love-building criticism by saying things like, "I value and appreciate you, and I want you as my husband forever, so I hope you'll try to stop smoking; I will do all I can to help you."

The magazine adds solemnly, "This criticism just might save a life."

This puts a heavy burden on you. Say the right words the right way, and you can keep your man from dying of lung cancer. Say them wrong and he'll smoke himself into an early grave. Brain surgery couldn't be more delicate.

But you are doing brain surgery—with your tongue.

"Accusatory language and curses have no part in the loving critique. 'I love you, but your smoking is disgusting and drives me crazy!' is a long way from 'I love you and want you to live forever, so I wish you could stop smoking, and I will do all I can to help you.' And which do you suppose is more effective?"

Probably neither. Smoking is an addiction. There isn't a smoker in America who doesn't know lighting up is lethal. In case your husband forgets this fact, all he has to do is read the surgeon general's warning on every cigarette pack. Yet, he keeps on lighting up.

But women's magazines still believe the pure love of a woman can change a man. Magazineland husbands always respond positively. If you read this article, you're sure your husband will answer your plea by getting misty-eyed, in a manly way, stubbing out his cigarette and saying, "Brenda, you're right. I'll never smoke again. With your love, I will fight this craving."

Magazine husbands never say anything like:

"Huh, what?"

"I'm watching TV."

"Look, honey, I appreciate your concern but nobody lives forever. I don't say anything when you stuff your face with half a chocolate cake, and that will kill you, too. I love you with a little extra lard. You can love me with my nicotine."

But perhaps I am being too pessimistic. Maybe when Don brought back that traumatic turkey sandwich, I should have been mature enough to say, "I love you, and I want you to live forever. If you ever bring me another sour cream and onion sandwich when I'm hungover I'm going to kill you."

Or maybe I need to understand that food is love. The women's magazines do. That's why we turn to them for advice on the most intimate matters. Women's magazines have always given advice. They tell us how to cope: with a mediocre marriage, with less than fifty dollars a week for groceries, with having to make our own meals and curtains and couch covers.

"Can This Marriage Be Saved?" is, the *Ladies' Home Journal* brags, "the most popular, most enduring women's magazine feature in the world." If men's magazines had this feature it would be called "Should You Bounce the Bitch?" Men's magazines have always behaved like a locker-room session in eleventh grade. Only the farting noises are missing. In the limited world of men's magazines, all men care about are booze, broads, and bragging.

Women's magazines want us to improve. They teach us how to sew, how to decorate, and how to cook like Oprah's chef. But it's not enough to have a healthy meal and a healthy marital argument. You must also learn to make hot, nourishing love.

The recipe for pepping up a vanilla sex life is not much

different from adding zip to a recipe. Take *American Woman* magazine. It tells how to have oral sex in seven steps. And they did it with such delicacy, it sounded like one more housewifely art. The article is called, "The Most Intimate Sex . . . and How to Do It Well."

Under the right circumstances, these instructions could sound sizzling. I swear they start like a recipe. Just substitute fettucini for fellatio in this opening.

"Practically all men love fellatio, if it's done with care and sensitivity," the article says. "Here's how to do it right . . ."

Like most women's magazines, *American Woman* makes the recipe so complicated I'd get lost halfway through. Here's step one for hot sex:

"Don't go straight for the target right away. Start by kissing his face and mouth, or begin with his toes, slowly, tantalizingly working your way up his body, avoiding any contact with his genitals. Lick his knees, the insides of his arms; suck his fingers, ears, and tongue; softly kiss his eyelids and nipples . . . Finally, when he's squirming with anticipation, concentrate on his sexual organs."

In this recipe for love, you're supposed to treat your man like you're whipping up egg whites. "Remember," the magazine cautions in step three, "the more saliva you use, the easier it will be."

It's not until step four that the magazine reminds you: "The important thing is to take your time and have fun."

Women's magazines are not big on fun. Fun is frivolous. Good women are serious. Step five quickly calls you back to duty.

Simple oral sex takes more coordination than a six-course dinner. And you still haven't been warned of the danger. Women's magazines always warn you about something. That same month, the *Ladies' Home Journal* warned you could get sick from your own toothbrush. When you put a man in your mouth, you have much bigger problems, as step five explains: "Maintain tight control to avoid choking."

You can choke unless you follow these directions.

"If he's moving, then grip the base of his penis with your fingers to slow him down—that area's a turn-on for most guys anyway, so he'll be getting even more pleasure."

And you'll be getting what? The Heimlich maneuver?

Did you notice that we're well past the midway point in these instructions on slurping the salami before the P word is mentioned? A proper women's magazine will go to any length to avoid mentioning that's a penis you are putting in your mouth. Mostly, the article calls it "him," as in "close your lips over him."

If you're new to this procedure, and had to read around the euphemisms, you might wind up sucking the guy's elbow.

But back to this recipe for steamy sex. By step seven you're testing your man for doneness. "When you feel he's close to orgasm, decide what you want to do. If you want, you can stop just before he climaxes and manually bring him to orgasm."

In a woman's magazine, there's no substitute for loving hands.

CHAPTER 8
Monogamy Is a Series of Adjustments

Monogamy is a series of small adjustments. You'll have to figure out who is going to adjust the furnace thermostat, the electric blanket, and the TV clicker. There can be bitter struggles over one twitch of the switch.

In the early days of monogamy, couples think these routine wrangles are ridiculous. Cold? Who's cold? You're both always hot. You can't wait to get back to bed again. You wonder how two people who love each other can fight over anything so silly. You find out when the first heat of passion cools and you reach for the electric blanket control.

Soon after we were married, our nights turned into a series of turn-ons. I turned it on. Don turned it down. I turned it up again. He complained. I turned cold. He was hot.

Just when I thought there was no solution, I read the *New York Times*. The answer was right in a Bloomingdale's ad for down comforters. The ad showed a couple of consenting adults under a comforter, regular price $375. (That's the price of the comforter. But the adults didn't look cheap, either.)

The ad was devoted to that important bedroom issue: Who controls the thermostat?

It wasn't clear who was talking in the ad, the man or the woman. But you can't fool me. I know it's the man who wants to keep the room ice cold. Anyway, the conversation in the ad copy goes like this:

"What's this, the world's warmest down comforter?"
"Pretty close, I like it toasty warm when I sleep."
"Toasty? It'll be like the Sahara in there. I like it cold and crisp."
"Cold and crisp?"
"Yeah. Like New Hampshire in October."
"Well, I guess you'll have to learn to adapt."
"Adapt? Can't we compromise?"
"It's my apartment, remember? I make the rules."

Stick to your guns, sweetie. You know he really doesn't like the room cold and crisp, like New Hampshire in October. He likes it freezing, like the Yukon in December. If he kept the room the way he likes it, you'd think you were sleeping in a drawer, with a tag on your toe.

And you're right to make the rules. You can't compromise on an issue like this.

When this couple marries—and they will, these types always do—they will discover that marriage has its ups and downs. She will get up about two A.M., and turn up the heat. He will wake up at 3:30 and turn it down. In the spring and fall they will alternately open and close the windows. In the summer, they'll adjust the air conditioner.

Bloomingdale's has the first sensible alternative to the old, boring arguments. Those are usually variations on this theme:

"I'm cold."

"Big sissy."

Now the couple has real ammunition. The new dialogue has crackle and snap. He can say, "I like it cold and crisp, like autumn in Antarctica. So don't touch the electric blanket, honey. It was a present from my aunt. Your family gave us the ice maker."

She can respond, "Tough, sweetie. I'm turning up the heat. It's my house, remember? Daddy bought it for us as a wedding present."

Soon she will be warmed by his heated protests. And he will be thoroughly chilled by her cold shoulder.

I admit Bloomingdale's solution is simply a test of economic clout. But what can you expect from a department store? Bloomingdale's may be entitled to its ad slogan: "What goes on in the bedroom is our business."

The thermostat is the first major monogamous adjustment. The second also takes place in the bedroom, and it's also about sleeping together. Because nature is perverse, one of you will be an early riser. The other will like to sleep till noon. You won't notice this at first because you'll spend all your time in bed. But the mating of late and early risers is a problem that won't lie down and go away. It leads to conversations like these:

"Are you awake?" Don asks me.

"Unhh?" I say.

I'm no live wire at home. But when I'm curled into a ball, my eyes are screwed shut, and I'm drooling slightly, that's usually a sign I'm asleep.

Another sign should have been that it was 4:30 A.M. Unfortunately, Don is a morning person. "If you don't want to talk, just say so," Don says, sounding disgustingly cheerful.

"I don't wanna talk. I wanna get some (bleeping) sleep."

"Okay," he says. "You don't have to be such a crab."

I do. I do. Our wedding should have told him something.

I wanted to get married on a Friday night. If I had my choice, I'd keep vampire hours, rising at sunset and sleeping at sunrise.

The time I met Don should have given me a hint about him: It was 7:40 A.M. at a college English course. Not only was he awake, he was teaching the class. I sat by a wall so I could keep my head propped up in case I fell asleep. The early hour gave our romance a dreamlike quality.

Our story is typical. For some reason, during the two hours they are mutually awake, late sleepers and early risers manage to find each other. Maybe it's natural selection. Couples stay married longer if they don't see each other often.

Don and I have learned to respect our time differences. I don't play the Rolling Stones after midnight, and he doesn't discuss Michael Mann movies before noon.

But I must protest a recent Gallup poll about early birds. I read about it in the morning newspaper last night. According to *USA Today*, 56 percent of the 502 adults polled said they were early risers. Fine. But then they made other, more obnoxious claims. They said early risers had more energy and more optimism. They claim early birds eat better and exercise more.

Of course they do. Every morning, they wake us late-night types at some awful hour. We spend the rest of the day in a daze, too tired to eat or move. After a while, it wears down our natural high spirits.

This biased poll didn't ask early risers the most important question: Do you take a nap later?

That's their ugly little secret. They all do. Early risers sneak in a little snooze in the afternoon or sack out on the couch after work. They may brag they're first out of bed, but they don't tell you they are also the first back in.

My own survey shows 78 percent of early risers have a

sadistic streak, especially if they have any position of authority. Corporations are infested with morning people. They
like to call 7:30 breakfast meetings for the pleasure of
watching the late show stumble in. Then, with all their col-
leagues backstabbed by 11:30, they go out for an early
lunch and let the late risers do the real work.

You can't convince anyone, but there is no virtue in getting
up early. For all we know, the early birds could be getting up
at five A.M. to go through our wallets. In fact, no morning
person has ever explained the advantages of getting up early.

Some mumble stuff about the beauty of the sunrise. So
what? A sunrise looks like a sunset, only backward. It's not
as much fun, either. If you try to have a relaxing drink
watching the sunrise, it causes talk.

The other reason for getting up early is even worse.
Morning people all tell you, "The early bird gets the worm."

My feeling exactly. And the early worm gets the bird.

The third major monogamous adjustment is an issue of
male control. If you really want to get a man where he lives,
grab his TV remote control. Many women don't realize what
a hold those things have on men. One man even gave his
beloved his remote as a token of his love. According to the
newspaper stories, he was a forty-seven-year-old car salesman
named Bill Lafey. She was Alana Swiec, a Massachusetts
politician, and she had lost in the Democrat primary. Alana
announced she was quitting her campaign for the legislature.
Her boyfriend, Bill Lafey, grabbed the microphone and said,
"Alana, you won me. Will you marry me?"

She said yes. She also said, "Where's the ring?"

The papers reported the dramatic moment: "Lafey spon-
taneously handed her the only thing he had at the time, the
TV remote control, as a symbol of commitment. 'I have
relinquished control of the clicker,' he declared."

Ah, the power of love. He was surrendering everything to that woman. I bet you one thing: After the wedding, she won't have a remote chance of hanging onto it.

In the modern marriage, it isn't who wears the pants—it's who controls the clicker. Even the most sensitive man hates handing it over to a woman. The clicker has an emotional meaning for men that few women understand.

For us, the clicker turns on the TV because we're too lazy to walk across the room.

For men, it is The Control.

No matter what else goes wrong in a man's life, as long as he hangs onto the clicker, he's in charge. I've always figured it was the perfect male symbol. It's long. It's hard. And I don't understand it.

But it's more. It's the last place where a man can safely criticize women. Jokes about our driving are out. Jabs at women in business are illegal. Complain about how she keeps house, and she's likely to hand him a broom. But a man can still complain that a woman can't handle a clicker. Ever notice how a guy will talk you through channel changing? You'd think you were dismantling a bomb.

"Okay, okay," he says, "no, no, wait, *wait!* Stop there." He can't control himself if you try anything tougher than changing channels.

We have four remote controls. They turn on the stereo, two cranky VCRs, and a TV the size of a Toyota. I can never remember which works with which. That doesn't bother me. I press buttons until something pops on. Meanwhile, I get interesting displays of sound and static. This seems to make Don a little crazy.

"I'll do it," he says.

"It's okay," I say, soothingly.

"It's not okay," he says. "You press the red TV Power button on the gray remote and switch channels on the newer black one. Then you hit VCR Power, and . . . here, let me have it."

I gave it to him. It meant so much to him.

The fourth major monogamous adjustment is shopping. Most women love to shop. Most men hate it. Monogamous men will shop with their women. But they do it only out of duty. The man goes along with it because he wants to please the woman. A man will appreciate the closeness and cuddling after it's over. But he doesn't enjoy the act itself. Most monogamous men just stare at the ceiling and let her do what she wants, waiting for it to be over.

It doesn't have to be such a joyless experience.

Recently, I shopped at a designer outlet mall. Every bench and chair had a martyred male waiting for a woman. The men looked like they'd been marooned on a desert island. They read magazines and scanned the horizon for rescue.

There was none. Occasionally, their loved one would come out of the dressing room. Usually, she wore some unnatural combination, like a suit and sweat socks.

"Do you like it?" she'd ask.

"Yeah," he'd say. "Buy it and let's get out of here."

Oh, sir. Those words are designed to make a woman uneasy. She suspects the worst: He's trying to get rid of her. She says the worst: "Are you sure? It comes in navy, too. Let me try that on." By the time she reappears, he's got a glaze like a jelly doughnut.

Maybe if I explained what shopping means to some women, you guys will lighten up a little. You might come to enjoy shopping. Someday, you might even initiate a little shopping yourselves.

For many women, shopping is a bonding ritual, similar to boozing with the boys. We like that, too. But many women have a smaller liquor capacity than men. Also, society holds us to harsher standards. If a man goes drinking, he's a jolly good fellow. She's a lush.

So we shop instead. We shop for the same reasons you drink—because we are happy, because we are sad, for celebration, for consolation. We call a trusted friend and spend many sociable hours pawing through the racks and shelves. We discuss philosophy, life, and love, just like men on a night out.

Shopping can be better than drinking. There are no calories. There are no stupid pickup lines. A guy with a beer gut and a bad toupee will not slither through the sale skirts and say, "What's a cute thing like you doing in a place like this?"

Most women shop sensibly. We buy a scarf and go home to our families. But sometimes, like men, we go on a binge. Then we face a painful morning after. We wake up with our slaughtered credit cards and wonder, "Did I really do that?"

In prelib days, sociable shopping was done only with other women. Men were brought along strictly as walking wallets. But now women see men can also be friends. We realize you are more than money bags. We recognize that you have minds as well as means. So we pay you the ultimate compliment of asking for your opinion. But do you appreciate it? No, you whine and complain. You refuse to enjoy the shopping experience.

Not that it's all laughs. Shopping, like drinking, exposes your insecurities. But bars are better at making you feel good. Their lighting is soft. Their mirrors are flattering. Store dressing rooms have the same decorators as police interrogation rooms. The light is harsh. The mirrors are cruel. You see someone who looks like you. But she's fatter, older, and has blotchy skin.

When a woman comes out of the dressing room, she needs your support. You can tell her if an outfit is ugly, but tell her gently. The truth will not set you free. It will set you back.

She may ask, "Does this make me look fat?"

Don't say, "Boy, does it. Is that Gucci or Goodyear on the pocket?"

Instead, look puzzled and say, "How could someone as slim as you look fat? But there's something wrong with the cut. The jacket (sleeve, skirt) doesn't hang right."

If you want her to buy it, say this: "I like it. But it makes you look top-heavy."

The fifth major monogamous adjustment gets you where you live. Or rather, where you don't live—in the living room. I don't want to stereotype any group, but some men have problems understanding the simplest principles of home furnishing. They like recliners and other butt-ugly objects in the one nice room in the house. These may include brass, teak, or mother of pearl items they bought when they were in the service and stereo speakers the size of phone booths.

One troubled husband, I'll call him Matt, came to me for advice on this vexing marital problem. He said, "Elaine, what's wrong with a recliner? I think it's the most comfortable chair ever made. My wife says I can have one in the living room over her dead body, which would probably make it wobble. Please explain why so many women hate recliners."

"Matt," I said. "It's simple. They're ugly. And if you want a second opinion, they're big, too. Fully extended, a recliner takes up as much room as a loaded van and has about the same style. The main difference is a van moves. A recliner sits there forever.

"Recliners are bad for your marriage and your physique. The moment a man stretches out in a recliner, his gut pops out, his chin sags, and his IQ drops twenty points. One look at him in that state and a woman knows Mother was right.

Some women slipcover the unsightly mess, but I find it difficult to make a man sit still while covering him with chintz."

Matt thanked me humbly for this advice. I told him to get his boots off the chair rungs. "You've been such a big help," he said. "Can you tell me something else? Why do women call it a living room? Margie won't let a living thing near it."

I smiled and shook my head. Men are so sweet, but so literal.

"Matt," I said. "Do cows wear cowslips? Are there monks in monkfish? Then why expect to live in a living room? The purpose of a living room is to impress your friends and intimidate your enemies. That, man, is living."

Matt wrung my hand in gratitude and wiped his feet off before he crossed the carpet again. He also sent Jerry, another puzzled husband, for a consultation. Jerry was nervous, but determined to seek help. He sat in my chair, crossed his legs, and played with a lock of his blond hair.

"My wife, Deborah, just bought a little table with Queen Anne legs," he said. "They're the ugliest legs I've ever seen. They're fat and bowed."

Jerry stopped and looked at me.

"Listen, Jerry," I said, "Queen Anne isn't too happy about them, either. But that's not what's bothering you. Why don't you just tell me?"

He took a deep breath and said, "Deborah wants wallpaper for the dining room that costs eighty dollars a roll. I said the Resale Barn had wallpaper that would do the job for five dollars, and it looked fine to me. My wife said all my taste was in my mouth."

It was a nice mouth, too. But I was there to help him with his problems, not make more. "I feel Deborah only wants me for my body," he said.

It looked like the woman made the right choice, but I let Jerry talk out his hurt and disappointment.

"I was okay when I scraped off the old wallpaper. But when I try to give my opinion, she ignores me. How can I get her to respect my mind?"

"It's easy, Jerry," I said. "Buy the eighty-dollar-a-roll wallpaper."

The man was so grateful, he couldn't speak. I was glad I could help him make another major monogamous adjustment.

Some men make these adjustments naturally. The rewards are great for those who do. Here is one example: If you're a guy who wondered how a geek like Lyle Lovett got Julia Roberts, I can explain. The answer is in an *Esquire* interview. Lyle told the writer, "There are universal truths about women."

"Oh! Let me hear one," said the writer.

"Women like to eat outside," Lyle said.

That is a man who understands women. As soon as the weather turns warm, we women sigh restlessly and look for a romantic cafe. We'll settle for six plastic tables on the sidewalk.

Many men don't have these feelings. They love air-conditioning. They think air, like beer, should be kept cold. No amount of reasoning can convince these men to eat outside.

"Let's sit outside," she says. "It's too nice to be indoors."

"Do we have to?" he says. "It's too hot."

"This is what real air feels like," she says. "We've been cooped up all winter. Why don't you want to sit outside?"

"It's full of bugs," he says.

"So is that bar you like so much," she says. "At least if I see the bugs outside, I can pretend they are passing through."

"What is it about eating outside?" he says.

"It's romantic," she says.

"Breathing bus exhaust is romantic?"

I could go on, but it's too painful. The man understands he has failed to pass another test. He just doesn't know what it is. It's not his fault. Many men are comfortable in caves.

Remember his apartment? It was even done in cave colors—gray, brown, and black. When these men go out, they find another cave. Men's bars are dark caverns. There are even some Neanderthals.

Women like light and sun. We are creatures of imagination. We imagine that if we sit on a parking lot under a Cinzano umbrella, we are closer to nature. If the restaurant puts out six pots of sunbaked petunias, we think it's romantic. A man can't imagine why we like to do this. Only when he is desperately in love—or lust—will he eat outside. So during their courtship, he takes her to an outdoor restaurant.

She thinks it's because he is a romantic who likes to do the same things she does. He thinks he's impressing her with his daring. It's the same instinct that causes small boys to hang from trees so little girls will notice them. But a guy doesn't have to hang from the tree branch forever. Once the girl is impressed, he can let go. So most men believe once they have done the daring deed and eaten outside, that's enough. They've proved their love. They won't ever have to do it again. Surely she won't make him spend the rest of his life eating outside, trying to hold onto his plastic glass and paper napkin in a gale-force wind?

Besides, eating outside makes him feel ridiculous.

This last argument won't impress any woman. She knows he is not afraid to look ridiculous outside. She sees men put on lime green pants and spiked shoes and stomp around the golf course. She sees men in short pants and sweaty Grateful Dead T-shirts running on the city streets. She sees men sit in cold, damp duck blinds at four A.M.

But these same men will complain that sitting in a garden restaurant on a summer day is uncomfortable. She wonders what's wrong. Doesn't he love her anymore?

She doesn't get it.

He doesn't get it.

Only guys like Lyle Lovett get it, which is why they get Julia Roberts.

If you survive these six major adjustments of monogamy, you're probably so well-adjusted that you can give yourself a little time off. A married friend told me when she was about to go through one of these periods of adjustment.

"My husband's out of town for a whole week," she said. She grinned wickedly. "I'm going to have fun."

"You can tell me," I said. "I've probably done the same things."

I listened eagerly as she began. "I'm going to watch TV until two A.M. and fall asleep with it on. And I'm turning up the volume to the level I like," she said.

"You devil, you."

"I'm wearing my ratty old bathrobe, the one he hates."

"Decadent."

"I'm going to invite female friends he can't stand."

"Which one? Harriet with the Hee-Haw Laugh? Paula the Politically Correct Person? Susan with the Society for Cutting Up Men?"

"All of them. We're going to drink white wine and talk about men. If the night goes on too long, they may stay over. We'll wear ugly nightgowns and talk until four A.M."

What could I say? The woman was born to be wild.

People used to believe women were a civilizing influence upon men. It was felt that without our gentle presence, men would turn into scratching, belching slobs.

Maybe that's true for single women. They seem to have character and discipline. They can keep themselves and their houses in order. But women who live with men use guys like girdles—for light control. When the girdle is off on a short trip, we snap back to our old ways. We crave those little indulgences we gave up when he moved in. Just for a week or two. Here are some of them:

Turn ons: A woman can fall asleep with the kitchen light on, the living room lamp burning, even the bedroom reading light on. We feel safer with a light shining somewhere. This drives men nuts. They can't rest until all the lights are off. That means we can't, either. These men wake a woman out of a sound slumber with, "Do you know there's a light on in the living room?"

The real question is, "Do we care?"

The answer, dimbulb, is a defiant no. Shut up and let us sleep.

When he is home, we observe the courtesies and turn off the lights before we turn in. But when he's gone, we live a brighter life.

Some of us also like to snooze in front of the TV or doze to the soothing sounds of the Grateful Dead on the radio or CD player. Unfortunately, too many men demand night-time silence. When he's gone, we tune in and turn on.

Put ons: Everyone, male and female, has some article of clothing their loved one hates: an awful T-shirt, a dowdy coat, a baggy sweater. Out of respect for our mate, we bury it in the closet.

When he's gone, it's on. We shuffle around in our favorite butt-sprung pants, put on our baggiest T-shirt or wrap ourselves in that reassuring ragbag of a robe. We wouldn't take out the trash in those clothes, but they feel so good around the house.

Disgusting little pleasures: Tuna out of the can. A drippy peach over the sink. Greasy takeout. Dinner at darling little restaurants where no self-respecting males dine. This is the dark underbelly of the woman alone. We revert to the meals he hates most.

Sneakin' smokes: Remember when you were sixteen and used to sneak smokes behind the gym? Of course, you gave up that dirty, disgusting habit ages ago. "I never smoke," says one happily married woman. "I wouldn't smoke in a restaurant if you put a gun to my head."

There's only one time when she longs for the coffin nails—when her husband makes his annual business trip. "Then I buy a pack of cigarettes and call up two or three friends. We sit on my back porch and smoke. We talk and drink and cough away. We don't really like smoking, but it feels so good . . ."

To be so bad.

But only for a short time. We know our rebellion will soon go up in smoke. We're too well-adjusted.

CHAPTER 9
Just Say Yes—Dealing with Your Family

This is a short chapter because it's not about success. It's about failure. My failure. It's about the one thing that really terrifies me.

I've always seen myself as fairly fearless. I've told powerful editors to go to hell. I've faced down crafty corporate lawyers and crack-brained cults. But when an aunt who is eighty-nine—that's her age and her weight—orders me around, I fold like a cheap tent in a thunderstorm.

I admit it: I am terrified of my elderly relatives.

Why am I such a wuss? Why can I stand up to mighty men yet cave in to a woman who keeps a concrete donkey cart full of petunias in her yard?

Because the aged ancestor is only doing this "for my own good." Those four words are a magic spell that render me helpless. Once my grandmother, great-aunt, or even greater mother-in-law start poking around in my life for my own good, my emotional age drops to about eleven. I whine. I lie. I hide things under the bed. I even run away.

None of these subterfuges work. I might as well be a department store display window. They always see through me.

The aged relatives commit their acts of domestic tyranny in the name of monogamy. If your family is like mine, it wants you to stay monogamous. But most relatives' definition of marriage is something out of a fifties sitcom: Monogamy means dreary conformity. They are constantly probing the state of your union. Why don't you have children? Why don't you learn how to cook? Who makes the most money? Does it bother you?

They're suspicious if monogamy is too much fun. If you enjoy each other after the honeymoon, you can't be seriously married.

Aunt Daphne kicked off the questions on our honeymoon. I didn't want to see her, but I loved my grandmother and she made me promise to see Aunt Daphne in Connecticut when we were honeymooning in New York.

When Grandma made her request, I wanted to say, "Are you kidding? This is supposed to be my romantic honeymoon. You want me to sit in a stuffy house sipping stewed coffee with a woman who acts like J. Edgar Hoover in drag?"

But Grandma said pitifully, "Please see her for my sake."

When I hesitated, she gave me her "I won't be around forever to inconvenience you" sigh. So I did it. But I made sure the knot was safely tied before I exposed Don to this elderly terrorist.

Aunt Daphne was the meanest thing in Enna Jetticks. Grandma told me she had been handsome when she married Uncle Charlie, but that was fifty years and one hundred pounds ago. Now she was a big woman with an enormous nose. I tried not to stare at her imposing beezer. It had red and blue veins like an anatomy chart. It had pores as big as swimming pools. When I looked away, my eyes went to the other part of Aunt Daphne that stuck out—her gigantic breasts, bulging under her blue-checked housedress like a pair of shoplifted pillows.

Aunt Daphne lived with her daughter and son-in-law. She'd beat them with her steely voice and iron will until they were pale and passive, and waited on her like well-trained servants. If Aunt Daphne didn't like something, they didn't do it. Since she didn't like anything, they didn't do anything.

Aunt Daphne didn't like that I'd kept my last name when I married. She set out to straighten me out the minute I walked in the door.

"Why didn't you take your husband's name?" she demanded, fixing me with a frightening gray glare.

"Because I'm a writer, and I'd lose four years of bylines," I said.

She frowned, and the dark gray eyebrows settled over the gray glare like storm clouds. That would have sent her daughter straight to the lawyer's to change her name. I sat unmoved. She was only my aunt, not my mother.

"We don't have any movie stars in this family!" Aunt Daphne thundered.

I thought the family could use a few, but I didn't say that.

"I didn't marry him for his name," I shot back.

Aunt Daphne was speechless at my disrespect, which gave me time to grab Don and escape with my name.

By the time Don and I returned to St. Louis, Aunt Daphne spread the word: I had changed. I was a smart aleck. Don was not a good influence.

My mother probed further when I went to her house to open late-arriving wedding presents. "Did you have a good honeymoon?" she asked.

"Yes," I said demurely.

I didn't say we'd had such a good time, drinking room service champagne at the Plaza Hotel and dining at the Four

Seasons, that we spent all our savings, maxed out our credit cards, missed the phone payment, and were now living on hamburger and the top layer of our wedding cake, which the caterer told us to keep in the freezer for a year and eat on our anniversary.

"What sights did you see?" Mother asked.

"Uh, the usual places," I said. The hotel room ceiling and the headboard. The rug and the wall.

"The Statue of Liberty?" she asked. "The Empire State Building?"

"No, we didn't get to them." I couldn't tell my mother we didn't get out of bed until after six most nights, when the Statue of Liberty and the Empire State Building were closed.

This interview confirmed the family feeling: Something was wrong.

My Aunt Louise made a surprise inspection at our apartment, which was three rooms over a garage. She made a shocking discovery. We didn't have a TV! In 1972! This was un-American.

Don and I prided ourselves on being intellectuals in those days. We would get around to buying one eventually. Meanwhile, we had plenty of ways to entertain ourselves. But Aunt Louise, who had been married thirty-seven years and had six children delivered by UPS, was staggered. This was not a normal marriage if we didn't have a TV. She tried to help. Aunt Louise took me aside and said, "Listen, honey, if you're hard up, your Uncle Fred and I can loan you some money for a TV."

The most persistent questioner was my late mother-in-law. She was small, smart, and round. She lived five hundred miles from St. Louis, in Marshalltown, Iowa, and conducted weekly telephone surveys to find out how I was treating her only son: Was he eating a good breakfast? Did we take vitamin C tablets to prevent colds? Were we ever going to save string, check stubs, and aluminum pie pans and behave sensibly?

She believed that if she asked enough questions, some day Don and I would turn into a normal couple. By "normal" she meant that Don and I would give up our slightly raffish writers' life, settle down, and become a scene from *Leave It to Beaver*. June Cleaver would stand at the door of our city flat and wait for Ward in pearls and a sweater. (What Ward was doing in pearls and a sweater is beyond me.)

Once Ward was in the door, I would fix him a nice roast for dinner. My mother-in-law thought red meat was the key to sensible living. She always asked what we had for dinner, hoping someday I would serve roast beef with common sense. We needed this for our own good.

It was too late for Don and me to change, but there was no reason why his mother had to be unhappy. All we had to do was lie. We used to give her a regular Sunday morning "It's okay, Mom, we're normal" call. This was a two-part performance. First, Don would give her an edited version of the week's events, leaving out things like, "The department store called and said they'd cancel our credit card if we didn't pay $86.59 by Thursday."

Then I would describe our mythical Sunday dinner, making up at least two vegetables and three courses. In truth, Don hated home cooking. This suited me fine. I didn't cook, but I could read. I got a basic cookbook. When my mother-in-law would ask, "What's for dinner this Sunday?" I would open the cookbook to the index and say, "Pork, Roast."

"And how are you going to fix it?" she would ask encouragingly. She always talked me through these meals.

"I plan to preheat the oven to 375, then score the roast with a sharp knife," I would read until I'd read her the entire recipe, finishing with "and then I'll cook it in a moderate oven for 30 minutes per pound."

It gave the poor woman peace of mind. It gave us peace and quiet. And it worked until one fateful summer Sunday.

While Don was going into part one of the phone call, I was upstairs cleaning out the attic. This was such a normal activity, it was the first item on his weekly report.

Suddenly, I heard horrible screams coming from the kitchen. It was Don, yelling at the top of his voice, "Elaine! Elaine! Quick. Come down here. The cat is riding a pigeon." At least, that's what it sounded like. I came running down the steps just in time to hear Don tell his mother, "I've got to hang up, Mom. The cat is riding a pigeon. I'll explain later."

I had no idea how he was going to explain that one. A huge fat red-eyed city pigeon was waddling in from the dining room. It must have gotten in an open attic window. Sitting on its back was our small orange tiger cat, Hodge.

Hodge weighed about a pound less than the pigeon. He was an indoor cat. The only bird call he knew was the sound of a can opener on a Banquet country chicken dinner. Some instinct told him to catch the bird. But it didn't say what to do next. So the cat sat on the pigeon like a circus bareback rider. No, it wasn't that graceful. The cat was terrified and hung on like he was drowning.

The pigeon wasn't scared at all. It looked indignant. It waddled into the kitchen and stood there. The pigeon looked at me. The cat looked at me. So did Don. They all expected me to do something.

I grabbed a broom, separated the cat from his catch, and scooted the pigeon out the back door. It sat on the porch for a moment and then flew off unharmed. The cat looked relieved.

Don looked worried. He had to call his mother back and

explain what happened. She laughed, but she never sounded quite the same. She wasn't reassured by our "everything is normal, Mom" phone calls anymore. She quit questioning us with her old vigor and thoroughness.

But at least she never figured out the Sunday dinners were in alphabetical order.

CHAPTER 10
Do Adults Commit Adultery?

Each marriage has one unbreakable, inflexible rule. This is ours: Don't cheat. We told each other before we married: If you fall for someone else, have the decency to get a divorce. But don't go slipping around, having some on the side, and humiliating your partner.

There are some couples who don't seem to mind if one partner sleeps around. There are some couples who seem to enjoy it. He screws around on her, she takes that as an excuse to fool around on him, and they spend the next several years happily hopping into other people's beds. But for others, the betrayal of monogamy is the worst possible sin. It makes the betrayed person crazy. Sometimes you read the results in the newspaper. He stabs her. She shoots him. He shoots her and her lover. She drills him and shoots herself.

But most domestic tragedies are small scale. The deceivers don't come to the kind of violence that makes the papers. They're gossiped about for a few months and forgotten.

One of these little dramas took place in my neighborhood, the ideal split-level subdivision, home of the good people, the churchgoing crowd.

Bill and Barbara were supposed to have the perfect marriage, although some suspected Bill had a roving eye. Anyway, Barbara never caught him until he started stepping out with Janey. And even then, she didn't catch him for a long time after everyone else knew.

Bill and Barbara were a handsome couple. She was slim and dark and looked ten years younger than forty. He was tall and blue-eyed and well-built. He was also six years younger than Barbara. This wouldn't make any difference to some women, but it bothered Barbara. She kept her age such a deep secret that even her own children didn't know it. It didn't help that her father warned her, right before her wedding, that she wouldn't be able to keep this man. He told her that Bill would be unfaithful because he was younger.

Anyway, Bill and Barbara gave regular weekend parties, went to all the church dances, and helped at all the church events, from passing the collection plate to collecting canned goods for the poor.

Their best friends were a couple called Jack and Janey. Jack was a quiet man who wore owlish black glasses. He was often the butt of Bill's boisterous jokes. Bill had a habit of heading for the men's room when the check showed up, and Jack always paid it. Janey was pretty in a flossy, country singer way, with frizzy blond hair that looked like it had been deep-fried. She didn't have Barbara's style or sophistication, but she was funny. You couldn't talk to Janey without laughing. She could sit anyone down in her kitchen and make her feel at home.

Janey and Barbara saw each other almost every day. They shopped together, had coffee together, and when things went bad for one, they both cried together. Mostly, they laughed a lot. They were like school girls.

Janey liked to have things fixed up at home, but Jack had no talent for building bookshelves or putting up cornices.

Bill was the handy one. He spent a lot of time at Janey's house when Jack was working weekends. First he was working on the rec room. Then he was working on Janey. The affair went on for more than a year. The whole parish knew when Barbara found out: She caught them together in a bedroom at a party. At the sight of her husband wrapped around her best friend, Barbara exploded like a bomb. There was a huge, public scene. The next day Jack and Janey's house was up for sale. They moved out of the neighborhood and then out of the state.

Barbara had been doubly betrayed, by her best friend and by her husband. Worse, her father's awful prediction, which had been hanging over her head for twenty years, finally came true. Barbara's rage boiled up uncontrollably. She was a geyser of hate, and she erupted into scalding anger, any time, any place. She took to following Bill around. If he worked at the church barbecue, she would drive over there, and scream that he was a bastard. Once, they showed up uninvited at a party at our house. Barbara and Bill were lovey-dovey, and I thought they had reconciled. Midway through the party, they started fighting. She screamed that Bill was "a lousy lay." There was a dreadful silence, and then our guests began making excuses to leave.

Barbara only made herself ridiculous. She was, after all, forty, and people think there's something funny about a woman's fury at that age. Bill became quite the alley cat. He told me church ladies propositioned him left and right. He also told me their names. I was shocked at the church pillars who fell for him. Bill said he loved only Janey, and he offered Barbara all his money for a divorce, but she wouldn't take it. She was Catholic, and she would not divorce.

I wondered why he didn't go anyway. I wondered why Janey didn't want him. I wondered why Barbara did. No man was worth this humiliation. Why didn't she have the courage to dump him? Barbara's religion was no excuse. I knew plenty of devout women who bounced the bum. At the very least, they lived apart.

I didn't know who to believe, or what. I did know I wanted to get away from Bill and Barbara, from his strutting and her outrage. I didn't see them for years. But I heard things. He had some deaths in his family. He took early retirement. He became sickly. He was no longer the strutting deceiver. They no longer fought. The marriage was saved.

When I saw them again, I knew the price they paid to stay married. They were sad, little old people, known for their church work. They were locked together, till death parted them. Part of them had died, long before they were buried.

What made Bill and Janey engage in a double betrayal of their spouses and their friends? The affair never seemed to be much fun. Sure, Bill enjoyed his reputation as the subdivision stud. But he complained to me that they conducted their romance in the backseat of his car and her basement rec room. I suspected they were both relieved when it was over and Janey moved to another state. I knew for sure they didn't find any way to stay together.

But isn't that what the University of Chicago survey found? Many adults don't enjoy adultery. Other experts agree. Frank Pittman, a psychiatrist and family therapist, writes in the *Family Therapy Networker*, "Most affairs seem to involve a little bad sex and a lot of time on the telephone."

That was certainly true for the only adultery I ever saw. I watched the uncensored tape of the Marion Barry affair: one hour and twenty-five minutes of sex, drugs, and dirty talk.

When it was shown on TV, the announcer cautioned that some of the language was rough. After all, Mayor Barry didn't know he was about to star in the hottest tape in Washington. Law enforcement officials planted cameras in the mayor's room at the Vista Hotel. There a temptress named Rasheeda Moore and an undercover agent called Wanda brought down Barry.

After what I heard about the Barry bust, I expected to watch a wild afternoon of debauchery. What a disappointment. What a snooze. I've seen more exciting infomercials. His Dis-Honor gave adultery a bad name. The tryst was a bust, long before the feds burst in.

Barry went for a quick turn-on almost immediately. One of his first moves was to flip on the TV set.

It's true he spent most of his time on the bed. But mostly he was making business calls. "Hey, what's happening?" and "Any calls?" are samples of Hizzoner on the horn. His behavior gave new meaning to the term "call girl." Rasheeda sat and watched him make the calls.

No self-respecting married woman would put up with that unromantic treatment. She'd haul her man off to the nearest marriage counselor.

Barry's hotel tryst had as much passion as a computer manual. Rasheeda didn't even give him a warm greeting. "You putting on weight?" she asks when Barry removes his jacket and reveals his mayoral paunch. "A little," he says. "About ten pounds."

So much for men turning to other women because they aren't treated well at home.

I guess I should be grateful the porked-up mayor never got naked. Barry removed his jacket, but that's all. He wore his suit pants, dress shirt, and suspenders the whole time. He never even loosened his tie. Rasheeda stayed fully dressed, too. They could have been sitting in adjoining recliners.

Who says extracurricular sex is more exciting than married love?

I don't know why I'm surprised by the mayor's lackadaisi-
cal lust. For unadulterated boredom, consider the come-ons
I've had recently. First, there was Uncle Vinnie. I met him
on a business trip to the Midwest. My friend George and I
had dinner at an Italian restaurant. There we saw his Uncle
Vinnie chowing down at another table. George looked
pained when Uncle Vinnie came over and sat with us. I figured I should be polite to the poor old duffer. I thought
Uncle Vinnie was at least seventy. Later, I learned he was a
dozen years younger. Uncle Vinnie had the physique of a
fettucine noodle. His form-fitting polyester shirt was opened
almost to his belt buckle, exposing a scrawny chest covered
with gold chains and gray hair.

Uncle Vinnie spent the whole time talking about himself:
how much money he made, how many men he screwed in
business, and how many women he screwed in hotels. Uncle
Vinnie was married, but he made it clear that monogamy
was not for him. He couldn't bear to deprive the female sex
of himself. According to Uncle Vinnie, women couldn't
keep their hands off him. Maybe that's why Uncle Vinnie
wore his shirt unbuttoned to his navel: He was saving
women the trouble of tearing it off.

When George went to the restroom, Uncle Vinnie made
his move on me:

"So, you wanna *Date*?" asked Uncle Vinnie. His empha-
sis on the D word made it clear he had another four-letter
word in mind.

"Er, sorry, Vinnie, I'm married," I said. I didn't add that I
wouldn't go out with him if I was single and had just spent
six months in a lighthouse. I wanted to be polite to George's
uncle.

"That's okay," Vinnie said cheerfully. "So am I."

It was time to be blunt. "I don't fool around," I said.

"What you do out of town don't count," said Uncle Vinnie, who was as ungrammatical as he was immoral.

"It does to me," I said.

Fortunately, George came back from the men's room, and Vinnie shut up.

Uncle Vinnie was a more obvious version of a certain nonmonogamous breed. These men try to warm you up with stories of previous conquests. Like Uncle Vinnie, they brag about all the women who go after them. They're never pursued by a woman who is fifty and plain. The women are always twenty years younger than the men and "good-lookin'."

I've never been sure why Vinnie and his pals talk this way. To let you know they're available? To give you a vicarious thrill? To let you know what you're missing?

I've also learned to beware of a man who says, "I think of you as a sister." That guy is thinking of incest. Ditto for the gray-haired gentleman who says you remind him of his daughter.

And what about the guy who talked about his family during a business lunch? He started by complaining about his kids and ended up talking about his wife. By dessert he actually said, "My wife doesn't understand me."

"On the contrary," I said. "I think she understands you perfectly." I certainly did.

Another variation tells you about his happy marriage. Soon he eases into an explanation of his understanding wife. She understands he needs female friends, particularly female friends who will meet him at the nearest no-tell motel.

I think my favorite was the high-powered politician who took me to lunch to discuss one of my more political columns—or so he said. Instead, he talked about his wife over an exquisite sixty-dollar meal. As the waiter hove into sight bearing a silver dessert tray with slabs of cheesecake and chocolate, the politician told me, "I really love my wife, but I don't get to spend enough time with her."

I said, "If you want to spend more time with your wife, why don't you take her to lunch instead of me?"

He called for the check and let me pay it.

At one newspaper where I worked, an editor invited me to a low-cal lunch. This was in the days before sex-discrimination lawsuits, when women were supposed to be grateful to have jobs. The editor saw me standing in the fifth-floor lobby, waiting for an elevator. He asked where I was going.

"Lunch," I said.

"Why don't you have lunch with me?" he said. "Semen has no calories."

"Sorry," I said. "I need something more substantial."

Don't expect any credit for turning these guys down. If a married woman is seen out with a man, people assume the worst. Even if they're only having lunch.

I needed an interview with a psychiatrist for a newspaper story. Dr. Marvin had a full schedule, but he offered to meet me for a thirty-minute lunch at the health-food restaurant near his office. It was the last place I'd pick for a tryst. The waiters wore sandals and had large, hairy feet. The booths had been recycled from a church, and they were just as uncomfortable now that we were in vegetarian virtue. We sat in the window, under the THANK YOU FOR NOT SMOKING sign, swilling organic apple juice and gazing at the recycled paper menu. Dr. Marvin demolished a vegetarian pita and told me about teenage pregnancy. I picked the celery out of my stir-fry and took notes while he talked.

That night, I got a phone call from a friend who had either developed asthma since I saw her last Thursday or turned into a heavy breather. "Sandy wants to know (pant-

pant) if you're having an affair with Dr. Marvin (pant-pant). She saw you with him at a restaurant."

"If I was having an affair," I said, "why was I taking notes?"

"Oh," said my friend.

It was a natural mistake. Two married people without their spouses must be doing something wrong. Sometimes they are. But I believe (and I have the statistics to prove it) there's less adultery than meets the eye. There are good reasons for our monogamous virtue.

First, we made a promise to love and honor our spouses. Second, we got a good look at what's out there. Mel Gibson and John Travolta aren't hitting on me. I'm getting passes from gold-chained Uncle Vinnie, beer-bellied editors, and boring businessmen. They aren't offering me champagne in penthouse suites. It's the backseat of the family car or maybe a six-pack at a Motel 6. The conversation isn't particularly brilliant, either. Uncle Vinnie's pickup lines creaked worse than his knee joints.

I will say women seem much better at pickup lines. The one who made a pass at my husband in a Capitol Hill bar didn't do anything crude like undress him with her eyes. Instead, she undressed his eyes. "Take off your glasses," she said. "You have beautiful eyes."

Don was easy. She had his glasses off in five seconds. She gave him her phone number. He was so flattered, he kept it on his dresser as a trophy. He was even more flattered when I threatened to rip out her eyes unless he ripped up her phone number. He happily threw it out. The encounter provided all the satisfaction he could desire.

Many single women are looking for husbands—but usually not yours. Single women say married men who run around are a problem. (Wives agree, but for different reasons.) "Like cockroaches, they're everywhere," Rachel says. "Married women stray, too, but they usually tell the guy that they're married." We're more honest in our dishonesty.

"It's bad enough to find out the man you've been dating is a jerk. But when he's a married jerk, it's worse," Rachel says. "We're not talking about married people who've decided to call it quits. These are tomcats who want to stay married but date single women. The real thrill for these men isn't being with you. It's cheating on their wife."

Just ask Sharon. It was love at first sight when she met Rich. He asked her to dinner and then asked her home. She went. She thought he was worth the risk, and at forty, she could do something heedless and romantic. He seemed to be everything she wanted in a man. Rich was a good talker and a good dresser, with a good job and a knockout apartment. Sharon stayed the night. The next morning, she noticed a wedding picture in the bedroom. It was Rich in a tux, standing next to a brunette in a long white dress. Oh. Oh.

"Where's your wife?" she asked.

"On a business trip," Rich said.

"You didn't tell me you were married," she said.

"You didn't ask," he said.

Motel operators also know this wandering species and its habits. A man who runs a rundown motel on the old Route 66 says he rents rooms by the hour to many married people. Too bad they're not married to each other. They stop at his place for a few hours of cheap fun. He takes their money and says their sex life is none of his business.

"People who know me say, 'How can you do that?' I say, 'Do you carry your marriage license with you when you go to a hotel? Who am I to challenge you? Is everybody who rents a room at the big downtown hotels married? It's just how many bucks you got and where you want to go. And we'll give you a reasonable price.'"

Besides, adulterers make better customers than honest married tourists. "There's very little theft. We have our names printed on the ashtrays. They never take them. They don't want to get caught with that in their purse. They don't even take the free matches.

"We provide soap, but often it's never unwrapped. My clerk couldn't get over that. I said, 'Use your head. You come home smelling like Lifebuoy, and you use Dial, that's it. You're in trouble.' My regular customers bring their own soap." And they always leave the motel towels.

Still, the most careful can slip up when they're slipping around. Every year after Valentine's Day, Dan Hill waits for the hearts-and-flowers fights. Dan has a city flower shop called Botanicals on the Park. Dan's shop has fashionable flowers and pretty baubles. But it's not in glittering Manhattan, where adultery might seem acceptable. His shop is in sensible St. Louis.

"About two or three weeks after Valentine's Day, we get calls from angry wives," Dan says. "The credit card bills have arrived. Their husbands sent flowers, and the wives want to know who this person is because it certainly isn't them."

Oops. He's been fooling around. The poor unfaithful slob was caught by his own credit card. One enraged wife found out her husband's girlfriend got seventy-five bucks worth of flowers from Dan's shop.

"I only got a twenty-dollar arrangement from the super-market!" she screamed to Dan.

Do these addled adulterers want to get caught? Are they saying it with flowers?

"No, they're just stupid," Dan says. "They're in a hurry,

and they don't have any cash. They put it on their credit cards and forget their wives pay the bills."

Feeling uneasy as you read this, sir? Here's something that should really make you sweat. "I'm not a lawyer or a priest," Dan says. "I'm not bound by any rules of confidentiality. If a woman asks a legitimate question about her account, I'll tell her."

Sometimes he gives a straying spouse a break. "One irate wife called and said, 'I didn't get these flowers, and I'm not paying for them.' I put her on hold and called her husband on his car phone. I said, 'I have your wife on the phone. She wants to know where those flowers went. I'm not telling her. You are.'

"Then I hung up on him and said, 'Ma'am, your husband ordered them. You're going to have to talk to him.'"

Here's another tip, boys. Don't say you bought those flowers for your sweet old Sunday School teacher. "Sweet old teachers don't get big, expensive bouquets of roses. They get nice plants and twenty-dollar mixed arrangements."

Alas, wives also get the cheap stuff. "Roses are for girlfriends," Dan says. To rub salt in a wife's wound, she'll have to pay for his philandering flowers. "There's nothing she can do. The husband's signature is on the computer printout."

One unfaithful husband hardly waited for his wedding flowers to wilt. "We did a big wedding last spring. Beautiful flowers, beautiful bride—everything was perfect." Except the groom.

"About three months later, the groom called and ordered flowers with a juicy love note attached. They were not for his wife." He was fooling around already. "My female employees sneer at him whenever he comes in. They think he's a rat."

Dan doesn't know the outcome of most of these domestic

dramas. If there is a divorce, the flower bill is never cited in the court battle. But he has been able to keep track of one man. "He always orders flowers for his girlfriends from me. He's had three wives in six years. That year's girlfriend is usually next year's wife."

But this year is different. "His new wife is sending him flowers. He's also sending flowers—to her. This looks good." Dan couldn't help adding: "Of course, they've only been married two months."

Some men try to make their affairs accountable. They get caught cheating—on their expense accounts. I talked with a woman who discovered the man she loved had put their entire romance on the company tab. She calls herself the Other Woman, just like in the movies. She says, "I want the rat punished."

The rat was forty-five and "going through midlife crisis. He took up racquetball, jogging, and me—all at once. He was a salesman and good-looking—blue eyes, gray temples, you've seen the type. Our office was one of his accounts. This started eight months ago. I went in with my eyes open. I knew he was married. I didn't want him to leave his wife."

The Other Woman is a thirty-year-old executive, pretty, a little plump, but as she says, "hardly home-wrecker material." She told her story over lunch, sipping delicately at a bourbon and water.

The wages of sin, she says, are lousy. No roses, candy, or shopping sprees at Saks. "He couldn't write those off. I discovered he put our whole affair on his expense account—the little lunches for two, the drinks after work. We met in parking garages, and he even put that on his expense account—under parking. He treated his wife even worse. They never did anything deductible."

This man liked some really weird stuff. "He said he

wanted dinner on the table every night. And he wanted his shirts *ironed*. It was time to write him off," she says, stripping the bread off her sandwich.

The Other Woman felt guilty. She lost a few pounds. She cried a few tears. The wife didn't look too happy either. The only one who was chipper and guilt free was the husband. "The rat was getting away with it. I wouldn't mind if he treated me badly and was good to his wife, or vice versa. But both of us? He must think we're saps. It's an insult to all women to let him off scot-free."

She crunched down on the last potato chip. "I blame his wife. All she had to do was look long-suffering and she could have racked up the goodies: a new car, a trip to the islands. At the very least, she should have demanded that he come home on time every night. Finally, I went to her house one afternoon to explain things to her."

You told her about the affair?

"No, she knew about that. I told her about the golden opportunity she was missing. I certainly knew how tough it was to get money out of him. I said a divorce was a little drastic, but if she wanted one, I would even testify for her."

What happened?

"Nothing. She's going to let him get away with it. There's such a thing as standards, you know. The rat ought to be punished."

She reached for a lemon slice from the pile of garnish and squeezed it dry. I reached for the check. "You have an expense account, too," she says, sadly. "I know all about those."

So do smart wives. The employees at one company are still giggling about the executive wife who called her husband to account. The division head had been fooling around for some time. When he went on a business trip, he took his lover. They went to high-ticket shows, ate at the best restaurants, and stayed at the best hotels. The company, which was in a budget crunch, paid for everything. Then one day the division head's wife called his secretary. "I know that my husband has been traveling a lot recently and taking me with him," she said, sweetly. "My lawyer and I would like an accounting of exactly where he went and how much company money he spent on these trips."

She caught him cheating on her and on the company. His wife was about to become his main squeeze.

You can always find reasons to stray. But there are also good reasons not to. A woman who was about to fall for temptation backed away from the brink when she thought it over. Muffy O'Toole is a slightly wilted flower child. The forty-something boomer was going through a bad time in her love life. Her once hot romance now seemed as exciting as a summer cold. There was nothing really wrong with the guy she lived with. But there was nothing really right, either. You'd expect Muffy to dump the man. She did think seriously about having an affair. But only her thoughts strayed. Muffy stayed faithful. Her reasons for choosing monogamy aren't the ones you would hear from your mother or your minister. These are Muffy's six reasons not to stray.

(1) **Too time-consuming:** "I don't have time for another project," she says. "I have a full-time job, kids, a house to clean, and a lawn to cut. I have very little free time. I'm not going to use it to sneak off and have sex. I'd rather save my free time for something I don't get a chance to do often—like read a book."

(2) **Too complicated:** "What if I get caught sneaking around? There are my kids and his kids, his child support and my visitation days, my health insurance and his pension. We couldn't just run away together."

By forty, you realize Romeo and Juliet took the easy way out.

(3) Too much trouble to be nice to someone new: "In my job, I have to deal with the public. I have to be nice to people eight hours a day. I'm paid for it, but it's a strain. When I go home to my current man, I can just sit there and stare at the wall for an hour if I want. With a new lover, I'd have to be on my best behavior for at least eight weeks, or I'd scare him off. I couldn't complain about my mother, my kids, or my job."

(4) Too scary: "We boomers have reached the age where we look best with our clothes on. It's difficult to have a fling fully dressed. When you start dating again, mentally, you are like a high school kid. Physically, you are like your grandmother."

Muffy is not ready to start seeing someone new, and she certainly doesn't want him seeing her. "I'd have to reveal my stretch marks, C-section scars, and torso blowout to someone new. I'd see his love handles and his sixties' knee surgery with the railroad track scars. I'm used to my current man's body, and he's used to mine."

(5) Too wasteful: "It takes six to ten years to train a man. By now, I don't have the energy to get a new one shaped up. Besides, all that are available after forty are used men. They've been partially trained by someone else, and then abandoned. I'm not willing to start all over again."

(6) Too expensive: "The overhead would kill me. I did a quick tally of the expenses needed to launch a new affair. Here are the basics: tanning spa membership, to darken those fishbelly white areas. Jenny Craig, for the saddlebag thighs. The Vein Doctor, for the varicose veins. Plus sculpted nails, WonderBras, and a pound of Youth Rejuvenating makeup. That's $2,000, minimum. I could just as easily feel the earth move if we went on a trip and I got a bay window for the living room."

Muffy and her man patched up their differences. She switched from checking out new men's pecs to checking out new Pella windows.

It's easier to look out than to look in.

And people will be looking in if you have an affair. About the only folks you may fool are your spouses. Everyone else catches on fast. That's why I didn't believe a word of that hankie soaker *The Bridges of Madison County*. There's no way they could do it. It's just not possible for a farm wife and a *National Geographic* photographer to have a four-day fling in Iowa without getting caught. *Bridges* is pure fantasy.

I was in Iowa about the same time as the affair between Francesca and Robert, or Meryl Streep and Clint Eastwood. By day four of that affair, half the town would be roosting like pigeons in those covered bridges, watching them carry on. Robert and Francesca might as well try smooching undetected at the Piggly Wiggly on Saturday.

My husband grew up in Marshalltown, Iowa. Marshalltown is no small town—it has twenty-five thousand people. But everyone knew what everyone else was doing, which is one reason Don caught the first bus out of town after he graduated.

We went back to visit his mother. I saw Iowa in the winter, the summer, and the fall. And the Iowans saw me. They are people-watching pros. If the CIA hired Iowans, they'd have no intelligence-gathering problems. When you walk into the town cafe, the conversation stops dead while everyone gives you a frank and thorough staring. That happens in a lot of small towns. But Iowans turn people-watching into entertainment. They watch you the way you watch movies.

I didn't realize this until Don and I went to the Marshalltown mall one summer night. The parking lot was packed with people. Some were sitting in their cars. Some were standing nearby. It looked like half the town was in the lot.

"What's going on?" I asked Don. I expected some scheduled event, maybe a speech or a concert.

Nope, we were the event.

"Iowans watch people," Don said.

They sat in the lot, keeping tabs on who went into the mall and what they bought. They noticed hairstyles, clothes, and things I wasn't sophisticated enough to catch. I was a poor city slicker, who only watched her step.

Iowans not only watch, they report—in amazing detail. Don's mom was a short, round woman who looked like Queen Victoria. Her pleasure was to serve us substantial Iowa dinners and then make sure we got a good night's sleep, starting at nine P.M. One night Don and I escaped and went out on the town. I had one Coke, and Don had one manhattan at the Tallcorn Hotel. We were back home by 9:30. Don's mom met us at the door and laid down the Iowa law.

"Maybe in the city you can carouse till all hours in hotel bars, drinking manhattans, but we here in Marshalltown, Iowa, get in at a decent hour," she said.

We were delighted. It wasn't often we were regarded as wild carousers—especially after one drink. What's amazing is that someone not only called Don's mom but also accurately reported where we were and what we drank.

This happened in 1972, some seven years after Francesca had her four-day fling. Now you tell me if she could get away with it. True, she lived on a farm, which can be more isolated than a town. But I guarantee the neighbors note every car that goes up those farm roads and when it comes back. And when Robert's truck went up the road but didn't come down, there would be talk.

Second, Robert the "hippie photographer" is supposed to

be staying at some tourist cabins near town. If he didn't sleep in his cabin, it would be all over town the next day. Decent people would wonder just where he and his truck were all night. They'd start watching that photographer feller even closer. And Francesca would be a prime suspect. After all, she was a foreigner and a newcomer, who probably lived in Madison County for only twenty years or so.

Somebody would see Francesca driving into Des Moines for a new dress and wonder what she was up to. Someone would see Francesca and Robert driving around, even if they did go to another county. They had to drive through Madison County to get there, didn't they?

Francesca would be wearing the old scarlet A by the third day.

There was no way Francesca could spend four days with her photographer and nobody would notice. Four hours, maybe. But four days, never.

Francesca has a better chance of finding Clint Eastwood in her driveway.

Bridges was badly flawed. It's hard for men to understand why we women all cried over that dippy movie. I remember watching *Bridges* in a darkened theater in Washington, D.C. All around me, women were weeping. All around me, men were wondering why.

"Is the movie that good?" asked my husband tactfully.

"No."

"Then why are all these women crying?"

I could tell he doubted their intelligence and maybe their sanity. But I am a woman and I understood. "It is the ultimate female fantasy," I said. "The women are crying because they can't have it."

"They want an affair with a *National Geographic* photographer?" Don asked, even more puzzled.

No, it's more complicated than that. *Bridges* is about an Iowa woman who has a four-day affair with a photographer while her family is at the Illinois state fair. Robert the photographer asked Francesca the farm wife to run away with him, but she won't. She says she can't abandon her children or her husband. Robert drives off in the lonely rain. Francesca writes down the whole affair and leaves it in the cedar chest. Her two children find out years later, after her death.

The story has everything a woman could desire. She gets four days of sizzling love. When it's over, she has another deeply satisfying experience: She gets to throw the guy out.

Most women want a little more than a one-night stand—but not much more. Francesca dumped the photographer right before the heavenly romance became too mundane. Robert will never ask her, "Hey, Frannie, could you wash my black socks?" She won't see him padding around the house red-eyed, unshaven, and hung over. She won't hear him making crude noises in the bathroom.

Four days is the perfect time to have the perfect romance. Once the glow wore off, would Robert really be more romantic than her husband, Richard the farmer? Consider some of their conversations.

Robert: How long have you lived in Iowa?

Francesca: Long.

Robert also asked her, Always this hot around here?

This is not the stuff of poetry. This is the stuff of long evenings in front of the TV. In ten years Robert and Francesca would be communicating in grunts. By throwing him out, Francesca gets to keep their love perfect, forever.

There's more: Robert has no one else to love. Francesca has a whole family. She really likes her husband and kids. She was just a little bored. Francesca has a nice sexual vacation and then goes back to her regular life.

Bridges is more than a satisfying romantic fantasy. It also has a powerful maternal pull. Francesca is a mother who gets to lay the ultimate guilt trip on her kids: "I gave up the love of my life for you." She also slyly lets them know Mom was a hot number. Very few mothers can convince their children they even had sex except for medicinal purposes. But Francesca's daughter is comparing her mother to Anaïs Nin.

Best of all, Mom has a secret until her death. Mothers never get to have secrets. Their daughters are always going through their closets, trying on their good clothes. Their sons are rummaging through their dresser drawers, finding stashed dollar bills and that hash pipe from college. But here's a mother who kept a wonderful secret in the cedar chest, then sprung it on the kids when she was gone. She wouldn't have to listen to them whine and complain before they accepted the affair.

No wonder women watch that movie and weep. We aren't soft headed. We're mad with envy. How did she do it, for crying out loud?

CHAPTER 11
Altared State— How the Boomers Changed Monogamy

It was a traditional Catholic wedding in all its warm beauty. The statues of the saints were gilded with pale spring sun. The stained glass glowed. The beeswax candles were tipped with soft yellow flames. Black-haired Betsy was standing at the altar in a white dress and veil, surrounded by six bridesmaids in orange chiffon.

Suddenly, there was a white satin avalanche. Betsy fainted on the altar. Passed out cold. She came to in a white haze. "Where am I?" said Betsy, beautiful, bewildered, and pale as her wedding dress.

"You're getting married," said the priest.

"Shit," said the bride.

That white haze was Betsy's bridal veil. She was on the altar promising to love a man till death did them part, which Betsy hoped would be soon.

"I didn't want to get married," she says. "I was living with this guy. I thought I was in love, but I wasn't."

It was an easy mistake to make. All the signs of love were there.

"He wasn't cute and I always went out with cute guys, so I figured it had to be love. And I liked ironing his shirts."

Betsy would have probably stayed with the guy until the spray starch ran out. But her family screwed up a perfectly happy cohabitation.

"This was in the early seventies, and nice Catholic girls didn't move in with men. When my parents found out, my mother had a nervous breakdown. My father called me a whore and a bitch and said the only way I could save my mother's sanity was to marry the guy.

"So I did. I knew it wouldn't work. But I had the apartment and the presents and all those people were coming to the wedding, and besides, my mother would go crazy if I didn't go through with the wedding. So I married him. It was the wedding from hell. It looked beautiful, but it was all wrong. We had a fight at the reception during our first dance. He walked off the dance floor."

The couple did not live happily ever after. They didn't even make it to the seven-year itch. They stayed together for two and a half years.

Betsy was no virgin, but she was definitely a martyr. She was a pioneer, one of the women who tried to change monogamy.

The boomers made a major contribution to monogamy: We've made it respectable to live together. Ten years after Betsy was marched down the aisle by her parents, most couples could cohabit with their parents' blessing. At least, mom and dad kept their eyes closed.

Now we call cohabitation "living together," a nice cozy name. In the fifties and before, it was "living in sin." Women who moved in with men were damaged goods in the marriage market. Unblessed sex increased a man's marital value, but not a woman's.

In the seventies, when the boomers started going to college, that changed.

Tom Wolfe was one of the first to notice this societal shift. He chronicled the case of Harris, who made a surprise visit to his daughter's dorm room, and found a couple going at it in his daughter's bed. Harris was stunned. He finally realized it wasn't his daughter doing the horizontal bop. Another couple was in her bed. The young couple coolly explained that his daughter was at the library. His daughter coolly explained that the coed dorm had set up a rotating system of Free Rooms, so couples didn't have to use a mattress on the kitchen floor, which was "gross."

If it had been the early sixties, instead of the seventies, Dad would have yanked his daughter out of that moral sinkhole and reported the incident to the dean. The frisky couple might have been booted out. A decade later, Dad looked dazed, but swallowed his daughter's argument. Wolfe writes:

> The idea of a coed dorm, with downy little Ivy Leaguers copulating in Free Rooms like fox terriers was a lurid novelty even as late as 1968. Yet in the early 1970s the coed dorm became *the standard*. Fathers, daughters, faculty—no one so much as blinked any longer. It was in the 1970s, not in the 1960s, that the ancient wall around sexual promiscuity fell. And it fell like the walls of Jericho; it didn't require a shove.

Wolfe doesn't cite a single statistic for this belief. But researchers say he was right on the mattress. Take a look at these numbers from the National Health and Social Life Survey.

For women born between 1933 and 1942, about 93 percent married without living with their partner. Most either were virgins or had sex only with the man they married.

The next group is different. It includes the first boomers,

the women born between 1943 and 1952. There's a drop of almost twenty points. Now, about 75 percent of the women marry without living with someone. Betsy was part of the experimental 25 percent.

By the time the boomers are in full flower—or maybe that's deflower—only 57 percent marry without moving in.

When some of the boomers' daughters start to marry—the women born between 1963 and 1974—nearly everyone is doing it. Only 35 percent of those early Xers walked down the aisle without sharing a waterbed.

"Our study shows that people who came of age before 1970 almost invariably got married without first living together, while the younger people seldom did," the authors of the study write in *Sex in America*. "But, we find, the average age at which people move in with a partner—either by marrying, or living together—has remained nearly constant, around age twenty-two for men and twenty for women. The difference is that now that first union is increasingly likely to be a cohabitation."

Shacking up, as your grandma called it, was more likely to happen first at a liberal Ivy League school. It was the early seventies when the dazed Harris tried not to think that his daughter might have copulated on a mattress in the dorm kitchen. It was also the early seventies when Betsy was black-mailed by her parents into committing matrimony.

And it was the same time that I was in college at Columbia, Missouri, almost exactly in the center of America. I was one of the women in that embarrassing old-fashioned 75 percent. I married Don the summer between my junior and senior year.

I was living in a semi-coed dorm. It alternated floors of men and women, but the elevators didn't stop on the floors for the opposite sex. Not officially. Ingenious members of both sexes learned to open the elevator doors.

When I came back for my senior year, the school made me

get a private room. Now that I was a worldly wise married woman, I might lead my innocent dorm mates astray.

Actually, I was getting the only legal sex in the whole building. My dorm mates were giving me tips for interesting new positions on my next visit home.

The hormones were raging during those discussions in the dorm rooms. But some social scientists believe Wolfe was wrong: The changes in monogamy had more to do with practicality than promiscuity. Young Americans aren't hopping in and out of a lot of beds.

"Most young people today show no signs of having very large numbers of partners," says *Sex in America.* "More than half the young men and women in America who were eighteen to twenty-four in 1992 had just one sex partner in the past year and another 11 percent had none in the last year."

So what's going on?

These social scientists believe Americans are sexually mature sooner these days. Haven't you ever passed a group of well-developed young girls and wondered, "Wow! I didn't look like that in junior high." You're right. Those girls have been eating their Wheaties.

"Thanks to better nutrition and other factors, biological maturity is younger these days," says Edward Laumann of the National Health and Social Life Survey.

We may be sexually ready younger. But we're marrying later. Laumann says the median age for matrimony used to be about twenty-two for men and twenty for women. Now it's about twenty-six for men and twenty-four for women.

"So now there's more than a full decade between the onset of menarche and marriage," he says. "People are sexually mature for longer periods. In the old days, they went to high school and then found a job. Many married right out of high school. A lot of women didn't go to college."

It's different now. "More people are expected to go to college. We expect women to have careers, too. People don't have the ability to make a marriage commitment in their early twenties. They have to finish school and get established in their careers. They are sexually mature people with sophisticated jobs and schooling."

A decade of cold showers is not enough, not even in the age of AIDS. One answer, we've decided, is serial monogamy before marriage.

These alliances have a life of their own. "Fifty percent in one year either convert to marriage or break up," Laumann says.

We may feel that we can choose a mate from anyone in the whole wide world. The reality is our choices are limited, whether we know it or not. Couples who marry are usually of the same race, within five years of the same age, have the same religion and education, Laumann says.

What keeps couples together?

"It's crucial to begin merging networks. If these networks combine, the chances of working out go up," he says.

If your networks of family and friends meet your man, say those deadly words, "he's nice" and nothing else, you begin to wonder if he's right for you. If your heart thumps at the sight of a certain coworker, but your cubicle mate says, "You'd never like him, he drinks too much," you quit thinking about a date. After all, "about two-thirds of married couples are introduced to each other by their networks."

Ruth and David could have stepped straight out of Laumann's survey. But they don't look or act like proper little statistics. She is bubbly and laughing. He is darker and more serious. They were introduced by someone in their network: Ruth's sister. They are both Jewish, and their religion is important to them. They found they had many friends in common. "I went to college with David's brother and didn't know it," Ruth says.

Ruth was twenty-five when David moved in with her in the mid-eighties. She'd finished college. She had a good job. So did he. Before the year was up, they were married. Right on schedule, just like the surveys say. But the surveys didn't mention the subtle behind the scenes goings-on. Even in this freer time, there were pressures and penalties for cohabiting couples.

"David moved in with me eight months before the wedding," Ruth says. "It was the financially responsible thing to do. If you're going to marry this person, it's time to start saving your money. Why pay rent on two apartments? Why buy furniture for two places? I bought the couch. He had a refrigerator that fit into the decor. We weren't engaged yet, but we knew we were getting married.

"We bought a rehabbed condo in my name, and changed it to our names after the wedding. David gave up his apartment and moved in with me."

It wasn't all down payments and appliances. There was love, too. And commitment. Also convenience. "Why should he get up at three A.M. and go to his place? It was cold without him. We wanted to be with each other, and we didn't see enough of each other as it was. Moving in just made sense.

"There was a downside. When someone else lives with you, it does away with your own space. But I could live with that, and I could live with David."

It sounds sensible and straightforward. Except when Ruth's mother dropped in for an unannounced visit. "We had to hide David from my mother. He would stand there in the closet, and my mother would talk about his mother. They didn't get along."

Your mother didn't know you were living with David?

"My mother thought I was a virgin. So did my father. David and I didn't see anything wrong with living together. We weren't out to hurt anyone. It was a private thing. We knew what we wanted to do. We didn't need validation. Our friends knew, but our families didn't. It would hurt them."

Even among their friends, there were subtle pressures. "There's a social grace period if you live together," Ruth says. "People expect you to be married after a while. A year is near the limit. If it's too long and you're not getting married, then you better move out and move on.

"You realize you don't have that many good years. In high school, it seems like you have a million years. In your thirties, you better find someone. And when are you going to do that? I'd get home from work at 6:30. How many hours did I have before bedtime? If you aren't serious about each other, you better begin looking again."

Fortunately, the arrangement worked for Ruth and David. They have been married eleven years. They have three children, two jobs, and a new house in the suburbs near Washington, D.C.

But what happens when it doesn't work? For Vicki, marriage led to living together. "I committed monogamy five times," Vicki says. "I committed marriage once."

That was enough.

Her wedding was not exactly a young girl's dream. It was about as romantic as a root canal.

"We got married at Russ's parents' house on twenty-four hours notice. The judge wore jeans and read from a mimeographed sheet. Afterward, we went to another couple's wedding. Russ was the best man. I spent my wedding evening at another couple's reception. We were dancing, and I looked down at my new wedding ring and thought, 'What a farce.' It was downhill from there.

"When you marry for reasons other than love, it doesn't work. It gets old."

In true boomer fashion, Vicki married the first man she had sex with. "I met Russ when I graduated from high school. I was a virgin."

He was known for scoring with Catholic virgins. Vicki was impressed with his knowledge of the wicked world. "He was a college graduate and a soccer star who bought alcohol for minors. He opened me to a whole world of college parties and illegal beverages.

"As for the consummation of our love—I didn't realize it until two days later. I'd been playing Trivial Pursuit with Russ and two other English majors. I'm a business major. I'm good at movie trivia, but the only author I can remember is e.e. cummings. I didn't have a chance. The loser had to down a glass of Irish whiskey with every wrong answer. After a few, I couldn't remember my name, much less some nineteenth-century author. I lost. For losing, they made me take a shower with my clothes on. Then I passed out in his bed.

"Russ had a bachelor apartment, but he took his laundry home to Mom. That's why, two days later, he mentioned to me, 'Ummm, my sheets had a stain on them. I hope no one noticed.'"

Stain. Sheets. Did that mean they'd done it?

"I had no recollection. It was like, 'I lost it? And I didn't even know it?'

"He said, 'I'm glad you saved it for me.'

"I said, 'Saved what?'"

Nowadays, we'd probably call this date rape. Seventies standards were different. Vicki decided her virginity was no great loss. "I wasn't saving it for anyone special."

Even when she was conscious, sex didn't impress her. "He was into Wet Willies—and I wasn't. I'm still not." A Wet

Willie is a grownup water slide. "Russ liked to put his tongue in my ear. I don't like saliva in the ear drum. It was his fetish."

But Vicki, barely out of high school, still thought Russ was sophisticated. As she grew older, her opinion changed. "When I graduated from college, I was ready to start work, get a nice car and an apartment. I was finished with him. I grew up. I kept maturing, and he stayed the same. He was still a party guy. He would always be twenty-two years old. I saw him sometimes, but I started dating other guys."

Russ wasn't the love of her life, but he was useful. "There was no place for advancement where I was working. He got me a job at his company. It was more money, a better bene-fits package, and more chance for advancement. By age twenty-four, I was a department head. We were still bounc-ing together, but I was moving ahead. I saw him occasion-ally. Then I accidentally got pregnant by him.

"I didn't get an abortion. Maybe I should have, but I didn't. I decided to have my son. His father didn't drive me to the hospital. My dad did."

Why marry the man at all? Vicki's company didn't care that she was pregnant. "They promoted me while I was on maternity leave. I was still on the fast track.

"We married for business reasons. My son was eight months old, and I didn't want to live with my parents. I wanted a house. I needed another income. We decided we were not children, we had this child, we were friends, and I wasn't seeing anyone. Why not get married? It was practical."

There was another reason: "Our marriage made the rela-tives happy. The heat was off us. Our parents pressured us to marry. Their attitude was, It's okay to live together, but once the kid comes along, it's not cool. Marriage was expected. I blame his mother most for the marriage. She forced him to marry me. I also blame her for the divorce."

Vicki had a mother-in-law straight out of a sitcom. "It was a power struggle for my kids and my husband. I was twenty-five years old, and she ran right over me. My husband kept saying I had to understand. He was an only child, and she needed him. She ordered us around in our own house. She directed the placement of the furniture. She wanted to make the baby's bedroom into her son's study.

"All holidays were spent with her. Most bitter was Mother's Day, when I had to report to her house for breakfast and stay all day. I wanted to be a mom and enjoy my kids. We had two by that time. Instead, I supervised two kids throwing eggs and then cleaned her kitchen and mopped her floor while Dad and Granddad were off with the kids somewhere. When we got home that night, I'd get a yard tool for a present.

"She got Easter, too. I never had an Easter egg hunt my entire marriage. She'd come to her door with a clipboard. She made the kids report each egg to her, and she'd cross it off the clipboard. 'Tell me which color,' she'd demand. 'Tell me where you found it.'"

It was a disastrous Christmas that helped finish the marriage. "I had to work until 6:30 one Christmas Eve. We opened our presents on Christmas Eve—at her house, of course. They didn't wait for me. The kids opened all the presents I bought them because Russ's mom didn't wait. I didn't get to see them. They had Christmas without me. That was our last Christmas together."

Vicki did not expect love in this marriage. But she did expect monogamy. When she found out her husband wasn't faithful, "I was insulted. I hated the betrayal. I couldn't stand it. If I weighed two hundred pounds or didn't wash my feet, if I turned him away in bed, I might understand. But there was no reason except he wanted other women."

Vicki wanted a divorce. She wouldn't have a mother-in-law or an unfaithful husband. But she might have an interesting living arrangement. "When we divorced, we thought it might be cool to still live together."

Russ's mother disagreed. "She showed up at the house and said to me, 'You need to move out.' She ripped down my curtains and stripped our bed of my matching sheets. She basically kicked me out and moved in, bringing her ceramic mugs, amber glass ashtrays, and those awful potted plants. She told my kids we'd divorced without asking me."

Vicki was finished with marriage. But she likes monogamy. Mike, a divorced man, has moved in with her. They have a baby girl.

"We split the bills, the baby adores him, and he's fun to have around. He can open mayonnaise jars and fix things. He cooks, and I love men who cook. He can do barrettes and pigtails for the baby, and he uses baby ointment when he changes her, which is something most men won't touch."

But Vicki still doesn't want that final trip to the altar. "I know many people who decide, 'We'll get married for financial security.' It's cheaper for me not to marry Mike. He has high-risk car insurance and a bad credit rating. His much higher income would raise my taxes. He declared paternity without marrying me, so my daughter has his health insurance.

"There's a lot I like about Mike, but I don't think I'll ever marry. But it's nice to have someone to talk to. I'll come home after work and say, 'I've got a new joke.' Or, 'You won't believe what so-and-so did at work.' And he listens.

"Best of all, I don't come home to an empty house. There's someone there, and the lights are on."

Although Vicki has "a roommate with sex," sex isn't high on the list of reasons why she lives with a man. "I'm a boomer, and we talk big, but we don't do that much," she says. "I've never really been a wild woman. I've worked my ass off paying for the house."

By the time boomers are Vicki's age—mid-forties—they know men don't move in without complications. They have children from another marriage, a troublesome spouse, bankruptcy, or bills. Love does not conquer all: Nothing may conquer his sulking teenage daughter.

A woman can get good advice about used cars, preowned homes, and secondhand clothes. But there's one used item many women know nothing about. Until you bring it home. I mean the used male.

I consulted Muffy O'Toole, the foremost expert on the used male. She had test-driven several before she took one home. She defines the breed this way: "A used man is at least thirty and divorced or split from a long-term relationship."

The used male may be the only kind of man available to women over thirty. This is both good and bad. "Many used men can be loveable, but loaded with faults. Often, their previous female gave up on their training and turned them loose."

You now have the doubly difficult job of shaping them up. You must help your used man overcome his old bad habits and instill new good ones. Muffy says these are the signs of a used man:

"A used man has trouble with money. His paycheck is spoken for. He owes child support and/or maintenance from his previous marriage. He likes boy toys." A used man has a state-of-the-art computer and expensive stereo speakers. The speakers are so precious he grabs them first if you yell "Fire!" His garage has ski equipment, mountain bikes, and a very fast new car. His answering machine has guarded messages from bill collectors. His mail has dunning notices from credit card companies.

"Used men have an ex. If your used man spends more time talking about her than you, he's still married to his ex, no matter what the divorce papers say. Even if all he does is badmouth the woman. Especially if that's all he does.

"Many used men have ragged underwear. Their ex bought it for them and they haven't shopped since the breakup.

"Used men may not want you to have children. They've had theirs, and they don't want to pay for any more.

"Used men have fears. They are apprehensive about commitment.

"Used men have desires: a clean bathroom, fresh linens, a person to blame for all the articles they can't find. Used men know it is the women's job to buy stamps, remember birthdays, and make them watch their diet and drinking."

There are used women, too. But Muffy says, "A used man is not like a used woman. Many used men like women. Many used women hate men.

"Some used men will try to train their used female. It won't work. Real women do not use ex-wives' recipes." Beware of the used man who asks you to wear his ex-wife's perfume, or says, "When I lived with Marci, we did it this way." Remember, if life with her was so good, he'd still be at her house.

"Both used men and women have needs.

"Used men desire a back rub, a maid, and home cooking." Even the strongest used man gets tired of a diet of microwave dinners, pizza, and bar sandwiches.

"Used men with children need another mother for their kids." This is a full-time need if he's the custodial parent. Otherwise, it's an ideal way to ruin weekends and summer vacations.

"Used women desire a maintenance man and someone who can brush off the door-to-door salespeople. A used woman knows a man is also a tidy excuse to bow out of invitations to Tupperware, Mary Kay, or Amway parties." You can tell your friend, "Gee, I'd love to go Thursday night, but you know how Gene is if I'm gone too many week nights."

A used man may not appreciate your efforts to improve him. "Old dogs do not like to learn new tricks. Habits such as power belching, eating in bed, and leaving golf clubs propped in the hall are difficult to break."

But not impossible. Muffy counsels firmness and kindness.

"Many used men have successfully hooked up with a new partner. With time and patience, a used man can even be taught to flush twice."

Forty years old, and you're back to toilet training. So much for living together being sexier than marriage.

Surveys show that by the time women are seventy years old, more than 70 percent will not have a male partner. Social scientists treat this as a tragedy. Maybe for some women it is. But I bet those survey takers never met some of the city widows I grew up with. You'd never get these women to admit it, but the day they put on black for their husband was the second happiest day of their lives. Love was long gone. They had nothing new to say to the man hogging the best chair in the living room. After cooking, cleaning, and keeping house for a grumpy old tightwad they didn't like very much, they'd had it with men.

These widows cheerfully put on sober dresses, sensible shoes, and had their hair done once a week. They went to church, played cards with their pals, terrorized their adult children, and decreed that Thanksgiving and Christmas would now be at their daughters' houses because they weren't cooking any more. They never let another smelly cigar in the house.

Now, they pleased themselves. They also secretly pleased their families. As boomers are starting to discover, when your sixty-plus mom shacks up with someone, it sets off seismic shakes in the family foundation. Susan knows this all too well. She hid the fact that her mother was living with a man for months. Then she met one of her mother's friends on the sidewalk outside church.

"So," said the church lady. "How is your mother?" The woman leaned forward inquisitively. Her tight gray curls quivered. Even the flower on her hat seemed to be asking a question.

"Fine," said Susan.

That wasn't what the woman wanted to hear. She straightened her hat and screwed up her determination.

"I haven't seen your mother at church lately," she said.

Should Susan say it? Should she betray her mother? Awww, what the heck. It was too good to keep secret.

"She's shacking up with Herman," said Susan. The church lady looked deliciously shocked. Susan felt better knowing the news was out.

Susan's mother, a proper widow of sixty-seven, is living in sin with a widower of seventy. Susan is outraged. She's not mad because Mom is having some fun. She's unhappy because Mom kept Susan to strict standards—standards she no longer feels are worthwhile.

"When I was dating my husband, Sam, I lived at home," Susan says. "My mother gave me a rigid curfew. If I got home late, I was grounded for weeks. Funny, my two brothers didn't have the same restrictions. They got to do anything. 'Nice girls behave themselves,' my mother said. 'We have morals in this family. We have standards.'"

She must have really cared about you.

"She did not," Susan says. "She cared about the neighbors. She'd say, 'What will the neighbors think if you're out all night?'

"When Sam and I were engaged I wanted to see him at school in Florida. My mother wouldn't let me. She said nice girls don't do that, either."

Once again it was: "What would the neighbors think? An unmarried girl flying across the country to see a young man. Disgraceful!"

Susan and Sam got married, which the neighbors thought was lovely.

Virtue is its own punishment. After their trip down the aisle, Sam and Susan settled into a life of responsibility. "We both work. We have kids and debts. Meanwhile, my mother, the woman who insisted I stay a nice girl, is happily living in sin."

What do the neighbors think?

"My mother says, 'They think he's so wonderful, and they want me to be happy.' She ignores the people who disapprove. My friends think Herman is weird."

The lovers would never make the cover of a romance novel. Herman is skinny, bald, and his upper plate flaps when he talks. Susan's mother looks like Edith Bunker.

Susan looks disgusted. The happy couple nuzzle and smooch when they visit her home, and she sends the kids outside so they won't see Grandma in the throes of polyester passion.

I couldn't help it. When Susan talks about her mother, the Geritol Jezebel, I start snickering. "Go ahead," she says. "Joke if you want. You won't think it's funny if it happens to you."

It's happening to many boomers. An estimated 166,000 couples aged sixty-five and older are living together without benefit of clergy.

This could be the last revenge on my generation. We've switched roles with our parents. We've grown gray and proper, tamed by debts and children. Meanwhile, some of our parents are living wild and free of us kids. The final irony is that Susan, normally a generous woman, knows she sounds as judgmental as her mother used to sound. She's turned into her mother—every boomer's nightmare.

What made Susan's mom stray from the path of married virtue?

"I think she's living in sin with Herman so she can get Dad's pension. There's some tax break, too. If I tried that, she'd say, 'What is money compared to your morals?'"

Besides, if Susan got caught by the IRS, what would the neighbors think?

Susan is more worried about what her teenage daughter will think of Grandma moving in with a man.

"It's embarrassing," Susan says. "I'm trying to teach my daughter to say no. And there's her grandmother living in sin. What kind of example is that?"

I hadn't the heart to tell Susan that if her daughter moved in with a man, it wouldn't be because of Grandma. The fun is just beginning for the family. If Susan thinks Grandma is a problem, an Xer's love life can be a real soap opera. Here's the saga of Sarah's friend, a college student who chose the wrong woman to move in with. The names are changed to protect these innocents.

"These two girls were best friends, Jill and Janey," Sarah says. "They went to high school together and they roomed together in the dorm. But then Jill wanted to live with her boyfriend, and he moved in with Jill in her dorm room. This was cool with everyone because they liked Dan, so they protected him from the Resident Assistant because it was a girls' floor and there weren't supposed to be guys there. The RA knew, but Jill and Dan were careful and didn't make her really have to face the fact. Everyone knew and nobody cared. Well, except Janey. She was still friends with Jill, but she had the top bunk."

It's not easy to sleep alone when a couple who's technically in your bed is in bliss right below you.

"Dan's brother came for a visit, and he and Janey hit it off. A month later, they moved in together. They weren't going to marry. This was just Janey's escape. Then he turned out to be a psycho, punching holes in the wall and stuff, so Janey moved out. She got back with her old boyfriend, the one she dated for eight years, and they got serious so she moved in with him, but they broke up and now she's with another guy and they're engaged and she's moved in with him."

Sarah does not feel that Janey is lightheartedly looking for bedmates. "In every case, except for Dan's brother, Janey thought she was going to get married when she moved in with the guy."

Sarah, a twenty-four-year-old marketing director with a lovely laugh and long, curly brown hair, has a different view of moving in.

"I had a serious boyfriend, Jon, and I wanted to move in with him, just for the summer. I didn't want to marry him, I just wanted to see what it was like."

Her boomer father objected. "My father wanted me to keep a separate residence. He knew we were sleeping together. He said he didn't care if I moved in with all my clothes and my underwear. My father just wanted me to keep a separate address, so I wasn't really living with Jon. My father said it was better to call Jon an ex-boyfriend than to say I used to live with that guy. Since he was paying for my apartment anyway, I didn't care, so I kept my place but moved in with Jon.

"It didn't work out. I was surprised. I'd dated him for two and a half years. We'd even lived in the same dorm. But we couldn't live together. After three weeks, we knew it was a mistake. I said, 'I think we should get my boxes and move me back.' Jon agreed. We broke up a month later."

Now Sarah is glad she listened to her father. "I met Bobby and he was the love of my life. I'm glad I don't have to say I lived with someone else before him. He was the first. I moved in with him. We're getting married in August."

Boomers created this living arrangement and suffered when this new social arrangement became accepted. Now their children use it, too. Moving in together is not really wrong, but it's not quite right. Couples still have to live with pressures to make a permanent arrangement that will please their parents and friends.

It's like Sarah's arrangement with her first boyfriend. Your heart is one place. Your mind is in another. And you're carrying a lot of baggage.

CHAPTER 12
Sleeping with the President

I could share a closet with Don.

I could share a bathroom.

A double bed.

A kitchen.

But after twenty-plus years there was one thing I could not share with him: a desk.

Don kept the pens on the left side of the desk. I liked mine on the right. He wrapped the pen holder with dozens of rubber bands, a guy trick that drove me crazy. He put in the wrong kind of pens. I liked thin, elegant pens. Don used thick, muscular ones.

He hated my habit of sticking Post-it notes all over the computer we shared. He typed his stories on my disks. I typed mine on his. We could never find our entries. He piled his papers all over the desk and shoved mine out of the way. I moved mine back and pushed his work aside.

I thought about divorce. But I couldn't find where he put the phone book so I could call a lawyer.

We were in a two-career crunch, the modern monogamous minefield. We liked living together, but we couldn't work in the same office. Some office. We shared a table in a cramped basement room crammed with a TV, VCR, fax machine, tape machine, computer, bookshelves, file cabinets, his easy chair, my exercise bike, and a cat box that always needed cleaning. Everything except the cat box had a thick mulch of papers.

We'd moved from St. Louis to Washington, D.C., for a year for Don's career, and the move was working—for him. It looked like it was going to cost me my job.

I was miserably homesick and worried about getting fired. It didn't help that our lifestyle went from luxury living to student slum with this move. Instead of a nine-room house in St. Louis, we now lived in a basement apartment on Capitol Hill. Two Congressmen and a White House speech writer lived upstairs. Homeless drunks roamed the alley, mindlessly cursing and urinating on the apartment wall.

Our dining room flooded with an inch of water after every rainstorm. The kitchen was so small, when I opened the stove and Don opened the refrigerator, we bumped butts. The furnace pipes rattled loud enough to wake us at night. The bathroom was under the steps. If you got up off the toilet too fast, you hit your head on the low ceiling.

But what griped my Midwestern soul was that this high-priced slum cost the same as my beautiful St. Louis home.

"Yes, but it's in St. Louis," sneered a Washingtonian, as if that was an answer.

"Yeah, who wants to live in Duckburg?" agreed Don.

I did. I pined for my friends. I missed my funny St. Louis neighborhood. That city seemed so sane after Washington's crazy traffic and chronic inconvenience. In Washington, it took a forty-minute Metro trip to buy a computer printer ribbon. A decent supermarket was half an hour away. Yes, we could walk to the nation's finest museums, but fossils and French Impressionists only nourished the soul. We had to get our bagels and Lean Cuisine some-where else.

Don was deliriously happy in Washington. He wanted more time there. Maybe I was down in the dumps, but I wasn't going to live there. One August evening, I came home from the Metro station with a drunk following me down the street screaming, "Give me your money, bitch!"

"Must be a congressman," said Don.

"He'd say 'please.' It's an election year," I said. "This place is getting me down. We picked this apartment because we had only one weekend to look for a place to live. Now that we've been in Washington awhile, I know we can find some-thing better. I'd like to start looking."

I also won a little more time from my newspaper, which gave me some peace of mind. The apartment hunt was on. The new place had to have enough room so we could have separate offices.

After a few weekends, I felt like I'd been in every house on Capitol Hill. There wasn't much choice. Most apartments were chopped out of narrow nineteenth-century town-houses. The main differences were how much old charm and new amenities each place had—and how well the landlord kept them in repair. In most cases, not very. I was amazed at the substandard junk these so-called tough Easterners settled for. Finally, I found an exquisite little townhouse with two tiny rooms that could be offices. I was charmed.

Don was not.

"I'm tired of these tight-assed townhouses," he said, as he surveyed the hand-painted eggshell woodwork. Maybe it did look like a doll house. But I'd found a bargain, and he didn't realize it.

"That place should rent for several hundred more," coun-seled a Washington friend. "Show Don what a really expensive apartment has, and he'll appreciate your pretty little townhouse."

I opened the paper to the For Rent section and found a pricey place a block from the Supreme Court. I didn't bother seeing it first. I made the trial lawyer's mistake: Never ask a question if you don't know the answer. In this case the question was, What does this house look like?

I knew the answer the minute I walked in the door. It looked like Don's favorite Irish bar. The living room had dark wood, mullioned windows and a slate fireplace. All it needed was *Today's Special* on a chalkboard over the fireplace.

"I feel right at home here," said Don.

No wonder. The main architectural feature was a mahogany wet bar the size of our current bedroom.

The owner was showing us around. When he heard Don oohing and ahhing over the wet bar, he knew the person he should play to.

"Look at this," he said, leading us back to the kitchen. "Two refrigerators."

"One for the beer!" said Don, ecstatically.

"And two ovens," the owner said.

"We can heat both pizzas at once!" said Don, revealing neither one of us was Julia Child.

We followed the owner upstairs to a master bedroom. It opened into a long hall double lined with closets. "Closets for both of us," I said, whimpering. For a year, we'd shared a single closet. Every time one of us opened the door, something fell on our head. The closets led to a huge bath-room with a Jacuzzi and an eight-foot ceiling. Even Andre the Giant wouldn't hit his head when he got up off the toilet.

I was sold before we even saw the two large offices and the guest room. We both agreed on this house: We loved it.

We couldn't afford it, but we couldn't afford anything in Washington. The tight-assed townhouse was forgotten.

What the heck. I knew our extravagance would pay off. I would feel better when I wasn't living in a slum. Things were going well for us. Don had just signed a contract to write a book. My department head sent me a memo saying I was doing such a good job covering St. Louis from Washington maybe he should send all his staff to Washington.

As long as we were both working, we could afford the place. We rented the apartment and moved in.

A month later, I was fired.

The trouble started right after the move, when I asked my editor for another extension. I was sure I'd get it. I had that memo saying I was doing a remarkable job. With computers, telecommuting was easy. I flew to St. Louis at my expense and talked with the editor in his office.

"I need more time in Washington for my husband," I said.

He said I couldn't have it. He said, "You'll have to choose between your job and your husband." I sat on his office couch, stunned.

"You want me to choose between my job and my husband?" I said. "Please don't make me do that."

"Oh, well," he said. "That's life in the nineties."

He sent me a letter three days before Christmas. Unless I reported to St. Louis on January second, I was history. There was no negotiation, no severance pay, and no health insurance. I was out after twenty-four years with the company.

I'd wanted a career before I'd wanted a husband. And secretly, I'd sometimes wondered which was more important to me, my husband or my career. Now I knew the answer. It was easy. I couldn't work for anyone who told me to choose between my job and my husband.

And so I was fired on January second.

There I was in the unemployment line with four other executive types. We were all wearing suits and carrying briefcases and pretending to ourselves that we hadn't been fired. We were all the same age: forty-something. We looked totally different from the young out-of-work folks in jeans and old jackets standing in line with us.

That's when I knew I couldn't escape my generation. I am a baby boomer.

In the sixties, I went to Vietnam protests, mostly on nice spring days. In the seventies, I wanted the Beatles to get back together, but I danced to disco. I still have a shiny purple pantsuit to prove it. In the eighties, I packed the disco suit away to dress for corporate success. I was a workaholic. At my peak, I held four jobs.

In the nineties, I was downsized.

I was sure I'd be the last person to ever get fired. After all, I was making my company a lot of money. But that's what we all say in those six-part newspaper series on downsizing.

But I am a boomer, and I cannot escape my fate. We've been getting the boot. The *New York Times* estimates 3,026,000 people lost their jobs last year.

When you're fired, you go through four stages.

First, you feel shame. You cannot bring yourself to tell anyone, even your closest friends, that you are no longer with the Figby firm. Finally, you force the words out.

Then you're ready for stage two: anger. You start by seeking revenge. You call the city inspector, the health inspector, and the IRS and give them the dirt on your company. But you're still angry. How can your company promote those useless losers and fire you?

Stage two is the worst, and lasts the longest. Rage gives you a strange, restless energy. Some guys can drown it in drink. But alcohol makes women fat and stupid. It doesn't work as well as a painkiller for us. Stage two may drive some men to work in the yard, mulching and painting as if it was their life's goal. But many women do something men never consider. We clean.

I don't mean we dust a little. We go for the Olympic cleaning medal. We wax floors and clean light fixtures and move furniture. In stage two, I developed a sickly interest in whiter tile grout and shinier floors. I no longer thought wax buildup was something in my ears.

I knew I'd gone clean out of my mind when a repairman turned up to fix a leaky ceiling and I saw his work boots were gray with plaster dust. I said, "Hold it! Let me dust off your boots before you walk across my waxed floors."

I got down on my hands and knees and polished his boots while the man stared at me.

That's when I woke up.

After my friend Laurie lost her job with an insurance company, she spent stage two cleaning furiously. She vacuumed twice a day. When her husband, Matt, tried to walk into the living room, she said "Take off your shoes before you walk on the carpet."

So he did.

Then she yelped: "Take off your socks. They've got fuzzies on them."

That's when Laurie came to.

Maria was another person who went clean out of her mind when she was fired. Maria took her last $200 and spent it on cleaning products. She snapped out of stage two after she alphabetized her canned goods by food group.

Unfortunately, Maria had already written that letter of protest to the cable TV station that discontinued *Gilligan's Island*.

After the raging stage two, bravado sets in for stage three. You've been fired. It's hilarious. You swagger through stage three telling people, "I've been fired" just to see the looks on their faces.

Then, in stage four, you discover that you enjoy being unemployed. You learn to survive on unemployment. You savor your leisurely breakfasts. You take long walks in the afternoon. You couldn't do that when you had a job.

That's when you find work.

After I was fired, I didn't miss my office at all. I threw away twenty-four years of corporate life like an old shirt. I'd had enough. I knew Dilbert was a documentary.

But I missed my readers. And they missed me. After I was fired, they called and wrote letters to the paper. They canceled subscriptions. They picketed in freezing January weather. Three thousand people signed a petition to get me back. In March I settled with the paper and began writing a column one day a week. By then, I had plenty of new and interesting projects to keep me busy working from my home.

At first I was surprised by the depth and strength of the readers' protests. But then I wasn't.

Most workers face the same dilemma I did: Choose between your job and your family. Most of us put off the answer as long as possible, just like I did. We hope we can have both. But we fear we can't.

Business Week recently had a cover story proclaiming, "Big Returns for Companies Willing to Give Family Strategies a Chance." The story opens with a Tennessee bank. After it put in family friendly programs, the bank had a "55 percent profit gain over two years." Other corporations with profamily policies reported lower turnover rates and absenteeism, higher productivity, and greater company loyalty. But that doesn't mean corporations are suddenly seeing the light.

Not if this survey is correct. *Business Week*, together with Boston University, surveyed eight thousand employees from thirty-seven companies with work-family programs. Yes, 48 percent said "they could have a good family life and still get ahead in their company." But 52 percent believed they could not do both—or they'd have to settle for "somewhat" of a career and a family life.

A sad 42 percent said their work had a "negative impact on their home lives."

And these are companies "with established work-family programs." They are making at least feeble efforts to help the sandwich generation who may be caught between ailing elderly parents and young children. What about the companies that aren't family friendly? They expect you at the office at eight A.M. even if it is your turn to take your baby to the pediatrician.

And so we put off the evil day when we make the choice by trying to please everyone: our families, our bosses, our clients. The result is a new breed of woman, the superwoman. She did not exist fifty years ago. The superwoman is not what used to be called a "career girl," a sexless office slave. Today's working woman is not a pathetic creature with no life outside the office.

No, the modern woman does everything.

All in one day.

You're probably a superwoman yourself. To make sure, let me describe a typical super day. In the morning the superwoman gets up and fixes her family a balanced breakfast. She puts a load of laundry in the washer, drops the dog at the vet, and heads for work.

She is dressed for success. Her tailored suit shows she is serious. Her silk blouse shows she is feminine. Her makeup shows she can't do anything about those bags under her eyes.

At work, she goes to a major planning meeting, writes two impact reports, answers fourteen phone calls, and drives forty-six miles to the branch office to handle a crisis.

On the way home, she picks up the dog. While she fixes dinner, she listens to her husband talk about how hard his day was. Then she drives one kid to ball practice and another to gymnastics. While the children are at practice, she buys supplies for their scout projects. Then she picks up the kids from practice, irons their clothes for school, and falls into bed.

Where she is a caring and sensitive partner.

A superwoman has only one problem parent—if she's lucky. Some of those fourteen calls at work are from Mom. Mother is newly divorced. The toilet is overflowing and she can't cope. Dad always handled those problems. Superwoman finds a plumber.

Dad is handling a different kind of problem. He's dating a woman two years younger than superwoman.

A superwoman knows a well-rounded person has time for fun. So she makes time. Her weekend parties are delightful. At least, that's what everyone tells her. She fell asleep the first time she sat down.

A superwoman always does two things at once. At work, she answers her mail when she's stuck on hold. At home, she folds laundry while she watches TV.

And when she finally cracks under the strain, the superwoman is still doing two things at once: talking to herself and putting straws in her hair.

Men have family problems, too. But working women have an added difficulty. Many men still don't know what to say to a female executive. A woman with a *Fortune* 500 company called me one day. She was furious with a male colleague. "How could he be so rude?" she says. "He asked me: 'Does my husband mind if I have a job?' Can you believe it?"

Sure. Some people may not understand the new office etiquette. They do not deserve our scorn. The poor slobs need help. Delicate situations are so easy to avoid, men, if you think about it. Just ask yourself this question, Would I ask Donald Trump that? See how easy it is? Only a twit would ask Mr. Trump if Marla minds if he works. You don't need to know who cooks or cleans the house—unless you want the name of a good domestic.

Nobody can know the internal workings of a marriage. But people sure try to guess. That's why the monogamous have to listen to mortifying remarks like this: "Does it bother you that your wife makes more money than you do?"

My husband answers that one with, "Hell no. I wish she'd make more. I've been trying to retire for years." He never says, bless him, that he's the one with the bucks.

I asked women executives about other difficulties they've encountered. These are real executives, not vice presidents for environmental concern at major polluters. Here are some occasions you may wish to note:

The business lunch: When you see a female executive at lunch with a man, it is impolite to assume she is cheating on anything but her expense account. It is also impolite to use the wrong knife on the executive's husband.

"I was at a business lunch," the woman says, "and I ran into my husband's boss. He could hardly wait to get back to tell my husband. 'Maybe I shouldn't say this, but I saw your wife at lunch with a man.'"

"That's okay," the husband says. "I know she eats."

Men should not overlook the advantages of equality. "I took a man out to dinner," another woman says. "He was my client. It was my invitation. But the poor man felt com-

pelled to reach for the check. It must be inbred in men."
Men should remember this helpful hint: When you see the
check on the horizon, just act as you would normally. Head
for the restroom.

Personnel questions: It is never polite to ask a woman
executive if her husband minds if she works late. Long office
hours are a sore subject with any spouse. Remember the
basic rule. Would you ask your CEO if his wife minds his
hours? She probably does. Unless she's working late at her
office. One woman gives this answer: "Whenever someone
asks something rude I say, 'How lovely you feel you know
me well enough to ask such an intimate question.'"

Here's another handy hint: When you walk into an
office, do not assume the woman behind the desk is a secretary. Even if she is, don't call her honey. And if she's the only
woman in the firm, don't ask how it feels to work with men.
One woman answers with a disconcerting, "I wouldn't
know."

An attorney says she is sometimes mistaken for a secretary
by people wandering into the office. But when her own secretary treated her like one, it was too much. "I fired her. She
knocked on my door and said, 'I can't understand Mr. Jones's
handwriting, and he's so busy I don't want to bother him.'"

Another lawyer, sensitive about his height and her position,
told this woman, "You remind me of my first secretary."

"That's funny," she said. "You remind me of my first secretary, too. But he was so much taller."

A man can be too polite: "I was on a trip with other executives," a business woman says. "We came to an escalator.
This whole big string of men stood aside to let me on. They
fell all over themselves. They meant well, but it was ridiculous. Their outdated politeness made me into a spectacle."

Equal partners: When married couples are partners in a

firm, do not make jokes about sleeping with the president. They've already heard them. Do not assume the wife spends her time typing and filing. It could be he's the cute bit of fluff with the great legs. It's even possible two intelligent people could marry each other.

"A lawyer was trying so hard to sound liberated," says one partner-wife. "He asked my husband, 'Does your wife work with you or for you?'"

In the marriage of Nancy Friedman, it's both: She works for her husband and with him. And her husband, Dick Friedman, works with her and for her. Nancy and Dick have two companies, Weatherline and The Telephone Doctor. "He's the president of Weatherline, and I'm the vice president," Nancy says. "I'm the president of The Telephone Doctor and he's the vice president. Some people have his and hers towels. We have businesses."

The Telephone Doctor is an international company with training programs for telephone skills and customer service. Weatherline provides weather and sports information by phone in more than one hundred cities.

Nancy is blonde, outgoing, and energetic. She reminds me of a sparkling fountain. If you follow that stream of thought, then tall, dark Dick would be a deep, calm pool. Before I start sounding all wet, maybe I should let Dick and Nancy talk.

"Dick and I started working together thirty years ago," Nancy says. "It was desperation. He couldn't afford to hire anyone. Then I thought I'd play mommy for a while. But I missed the business world. I wasn't happy with changing diapers and making conversations with mothers on the playground. I said, 'I need to go out and work.' He said, 'You'll work for me. You're too talented to work for anyone else.'"

Amazing. Thirty years ago, men still said things like, "No

wife of mine works," and got away with it. Dick didn't. "He has a deep respect for my decisions and opinions. It's why we work so well together."

But it's mutual. Nancy admires her husband's talent, too.

"He taught me to sell radio time. That's the hardest thing to sell. You're selling a box of air: You can't show it. You can't feel it. You can't see it. And it's gone before you know it. I was one of the first female sales reps, selling at a radio station we owned.

"Then we sold the radio station and started the Weatherline business. I worked there under the name Nancy Miller, so it didn't sound like a ma and pa business. This went on for years. Most people had no idea Dick and I were married. He was always hearing, 'That Nancy Miller is fantastic.'

"When Dick traveled, clients would tell me, 'Dick was in town last night. What a fun guy. Oh, boy, can Dick drink!'"

The whole concept crumbled with one offhand comment from Nancy.

"An old client said to me, 'You are great. How does Dick treat you?'

"I said, 'Well, I get to sleep with him.'

"There was a shocked silence. The client said, 'Pardon me?'

"He'd worked with us for four years and didn't realize we were married. After that, I had to come out of the closet. I told everyone Dick kept it quiet for so long because he was ashamed of me."

The Friedmans' biggest problem? They both agree about that: When does work end?

"Dick can turn it off at six o'clock when he walks out the door. I cannot. My mind is racing about the business all the time. We made a rule. We don't talk business after work. I can usually keep it until about eight P.M. Then I'll say, 'Dick, do you think we should . . .' This is a one-sided rule, any-way. If by chance he wants to talk about work after six P.M., it's okay. That's his executive prerogative."

Dick has his own feelings about couples who work together. "If done well, it strengthens the marriage," he says. "You experience the highs and lows together. It saves rehashing the day to a nonworking partner. And you can hold board meetings in a telephone booth."

The cons?

"Working together can also weaken a marriage. I've had lots of husbands and wives say it takes a while to learn that your disagreements in business stay at work. You have to prevent the emotional leakage into your home life.

"Plus, it would be very hard to have an affair at the office."

There was a long pause. Then Dick adds, "I'd like to say I truly speak from lack of experience."

Lorraine Dieckmeyer worked with her husband Bud for more than twenty years. She was the brains of the family business. But she stayed back in the kitchen. She had to. Lorraine fried up the brain sandwiches, house specialty of Dieckmeyer's Bar & Restaurant in south St. Louis. That's the old German section of St. Louis. The Germans never wasted anything. They either fried it or put sugar on it, or sometimes both. Brain sandwiches are crispy, deep-fat-fried cow brains, served on a bun with a slice of Bermuda onion and washed down with cold beer.

McDonald's probably won't be putting a McBrain on the menu. But that didn't bother the Dieckmeyers. Their saloon attracted brain lovers from Alaska to Florida. Bud and Lorraine's brains were so famous, their restaurant was featured in *USA Today*, and on national radio and television shows. BBC-TV did a story about them. Even people who wouldn't eat brain sandwiches are fascinated by the thought of them.

If you think brains are disgusting to eat, you should try fixing them. The preparation resembles an autopsy. The secret isn't in the sauce. Blood in the brains makes them taste bitter. You have to soak them in salt water and remove the membrane. "I dreaded that membrane, and I hated cleaning those babies all the time," Lorraine says. "I've got someone else to do the cleaning now."

Lorraine made another major change in the family business. I'll tell you about that. But first, you must understand that she and Bud married in 1948, and they had a traditional marriage. Bud was a German bartender of the old school: honest, hardworking, and hardheaded.

Bud and Lorraine belonged to a tough breed, much tougher than my generation. "We raised five kids in a three-room flat," she says. "Plus we inherited his mother. She had two rooms in the flat on the other side. When Bud's dad died, she was scared to be alone, so we broke a door through to our place for her. After twenty-five years we saved enough money for our house, and I thought I'd died and went to heaven. I could hang out my laundry without his mother knowing about it.

"Friday was my rough day when I cooked. I'd set up the kitchen at eight in the morning and work until past lunch, about two P.M. We'd rest for about two hours in the afternoon and be back at the bar by five. We'd stay open until 1:30 in the morning. The rest of the time, I'd go in at lunchtime, go home after lunch, and then come back at five and work until 1:30 A.M."

Bud drove himself just as hard.

"You can't be sick when you're married to the boss. I'd wake up some mornings and say, 'I feel so bad, I can't go in.'

And Bud would say, 'Can't you just make it through lunch?'
And I'd get up and go in and work all day.

"I guess I was back in that kitchen a long time, sweating
my brains out." (Lorraine is immune to all brain puns by
now.) "Finally, I said I'd like to get out in front. Bud said, 'I
don't know about that.'

"But I did. They had a class for assertiveness at the local
grade school. I took it—lasted for six weeks. Finally, I
worked my way out to the front. I cooked at lunchtime and
waited tables at night and that's when he went into the back
and cooked. Bud hated it. But he had no alternative. It was
my turn."

Lorraine didn't always enjoy working, but she did enjoy
Bud. He was a big healthy man, and it was a shock when
the doctor said he had cancer of the esophagus. "He went
fast," she says. "And he went to work, even if it was only for
an hour, right up to the end. I really miss him. It's lonesome
at night."

It's a lot of worry by day. Bud handled the house repairs
in their marriage. Lorraine took care of the cleaning. "Now
I'm worrying about the mold on the siding and who to call
when the air conditioning breaks. Bud did all that, and I
don't know what I'm doing.

"The kids want me to move in with them, but I know
that trap. I'd be a free baby-sitter. Then the kids say, 'Why
don't you meet someone for companionship?' I've already
had one proposal of marriage. This guy says, 'Wanna get
married?' He's younger than me, but he weighs three hundred pounds. I thought, 'Oh, no, he don't want me. He's
looking for a cook.' Besides, he'd squash me, if you know
what I mean. And I'm not washing laundry the size of a
tent."

So Lorraine said no. And did what she's always done. She

went to work. "I think people who sit at home grow old," she says.

She opened the restaurant again after Bud's death with the help of her two youngest children. But you'll notice a slight difference from the days when Lorraine cooked and Bud tended bar. Now her daughter Nancy is out front. Her son John is the cook. He's in back.

And Lorraine?

She's still the brains of the operation.

Monogamy Is Not for Sissies

"We're going on a vacation," I told my friend Ruth.

"It's about time," she said. "Where are you going?"

"To an inn near St. Michael's on the Chesapeake Bay."

"What are you doing there?" said Ruth.

"Nothing," I said.

"What's that mean?" said Ruth.

Good question. Why did I say "nothing" when I meant "everything"?

"Nothing is Catholic for screw," I said.

Ruth giggled. "Good. I was worried you really were going to do nothing."

"Did you really have to use that word?" I could hear Sister Mary Michael asking. Long after I left Catholic school, she was still with me, censoring my impure thoughts. A word like that had to be at least a penance of five Our Fathers and five Hail Marys. The married women I grew up around might say "make love" but they'd purse their mouths to show it wasn't nearly as wholesome as making dinner.

Yes, sister. I do have to talk that way. I've taken my first militantly monogamous step. I've declared married people like recreational sex. Why did you think we married? So I could sort his socks and he could take out the trash?

But I knew Ozzie and Harriet would fall out of their twin beds at talk like that. The women in my mother's coffee circle would drop their cups. They'd never say that to their female friends. But they'd tell them everything else. I'd sat at my listening post by the furnace grate on my bedroom floor and heard them cry over their unwanted pregnancies. I knew their husbands were lousy lovers, and the details would make the *Playboy* Advisor blush.

The coffee circle women might brag if their husbands got a promotion, built a new patio, or bought them a nice anniversary present. But I'd never heard them say anything good about their love lives. Were their husbands always such awful lovers? Or did these women talk that way because a proper married woman was supposed to? Just like she was supposed to have her hair done at the beauty shop one day a week. I didn't want to sleep in neck-cramping style on a satin pillow to preserve my hairdo all week. And I didn't want to tell my man, "Okay, you can do it, but don't mess up my hair."

But I have my wifely duty: not to sound like a sitcom wife. It's time we married people quit creeping around like marriage is an embarrassing condition. No wonder folks think monogamy is dull. We act like committing monogamy is a shameful act. Single people brag all the time, and they have much less to brag about. We need to acquire the same single mindedness for the married state.

Now, I ask myself this question, What would I say if Don and I were single? If we were having an affair, I'd have told Ruth we were going away together. Heck, I'd have been proud of it. Instead, when I was caught *in flagrante* with my husband, I gave Ruth a mealy-mouthed answer. Never again.

We marrieds have a national average to maintain, and singles are just too unreliable to keep the . . . numbers . . . up.

Might as well admit it. Most of us have been monogamous all along. Even in the sixties, we boomers weren't as wild as we pretended to be. Despite our big talk, most of us didn't move in with a guy unless we were engaged. Our pre-AIDS sex lives—what we remember of them through the drugs—were overrated. Even the Doors' Jim Morrison only did it twice a week. Didn't he sing that you should love him two times and last him all through the week? Jim Morrison did it twice a week, just like the surveys said.

Yeah, sure, there are wives who sleep in curlers and husbands who take after-supper naps in their recliners so they won't be too tired when they go to bed. But I still believe that quietly, carefully, household by household, monogamy is being transformed into something slightly shocking, by doing the unexpected.

Consider Elmer, a boomer with a naked desire: He wanted to see if he could go two weeks without going to the tavern. So Elmer made a deal with his wife, Charlene.

"It was just a whim," he says.

People in Elmer's neighborhood do not have whims. They have bills and children. But Elmer didn't want a Porsche or a pinkie ring. Elmer wanted to go to a nudist resort. Not for any funny business, mind you. Elmer wanted to spend the day at a respectable resort, swimming, picnicking, and doing whatever respectable people do without their clothes.

Elmer made Charlene this deal: If she'd take off her clothes for one day, he'd stay out of the saloon for two solid weeks. Fourteen days to one seemed a fair trade to him. It seemed fair to Charlene, too. She agreed to undress for success.

If Elmer's request surprised her, she surprised him right back.

Elmer found a nudist resort deep in the Midwest woods. The resort sent Elmer a map and a date to visit. So Elmer, a forty-six-year-old guy who drives a truck, and Charlene, who works for a temp service, set off on their adventure with nothing but two towels. "We had no courage-bolstering beverages," Elmer says. "The only liquid in our vehicle was an industrial-size jug of sunscreen."

The resort was about forty-five minutes away. "We could never find it without their map, and that's how they want it. The main entrance was a neatly landscaped opening in the woods. A sign on a telephone pole directed us to 'ring bell and wait.' Within minutes we were met by an older couple, casually dressed."

Elmer was reassured. "The woman was a homey person. She looked a lot like Aunt Bea." Just the sort of person you could set a spell and take off your clothes with.

"The couple unlocked the gate and led us to the office for check-in and the inevitable disrobing. For a few moments, I thought I would be overcome with an attack of modesty. I wondered if Charlene was as nervous as I was. I turned around, and she was already sporting her birthday suit."

"Get a move on," Charlene said.

"When we walked outside together the nervousness all but disappeared. We were just like everyone else, except for our lack of tan." Elmer now understood why new nudists were called cotton tails.

"There were no fashion statements there. It's unusual walking around with nothing on but a pair of shoes. The people were very friendly and very brown. They had stuff tanned on them the sun doesn't usually see."

How can I put this delicately? When you met someone attractive, were you sorry you weren't wearing clothes?

"It's not like that," Elmer says. "It's not a girlie joint."

"It's not about sex," Charlene says. "It's about freedom. It was a nice afternoon. Nobody pointed and laughed at us. I wasn't embarrassed because everyone was like me."

The resort had a pond, a pool, campgrounds, and hiking trails. Aunt Bea warned them about ticks on the trails. "We stuck to the pool," Elmer says. "As we basked in the sun, Charlene snickered, 'When does your tavern-free two weeks begin?' "

Elmer kept his deal and barred himself. After fourteen days of sober reflection, he says his nudist experience was "peaceful, unique, and exhilarating. We've talked about going back again, but we'll have to make it soon. I don't want to go there when it's cold."

Naturally. The resort would be clothed for the season.

Maybe there aren't enough husbands like Elmer to make their mark statistically. But they're out there, where you'd least expect, making those unexpected requests that can save a marriage. Conformity is the great enemy of monogamy. Too many eye-glazing dinners at the in-laws may kill as many marriages as the other woman (or man). Yet too many husbands and wives feel obligated to go to their in-laws weekend after weekend, until the stone dullness grinds away their marriage.

It took a married man to find a way out of this trap. His name is Ray, and he discovered the Law of the Lifetime Remainder. Ray's finding could help revitalize monogamy. Like many great discoveries, it began with an ordinary event. Newton discovered gravity when he was bonked on the head with an apple. Ray's inspiration came from the potato. The couch potato.

Ray was having a discussion with his wife. She wanted to spend a weekend in some dull, unfamiliar place. He looked forward to a restorative snooze on the couch. "It's only one weekend," said his wife. But Ray knew it would be one long weekend. He began to calculate what that weekend was worth. "I'm pushing forty," he says. "With any luck, I'll live another thirty years. That means I only have about fifteen hundred weekends left. I don't want to waste one."

That chilling number gave Ray the strength to refuse. There was barely time to do all the things he wanted. The Law of the Lifetime Remainder was born. Ray's law says life is too short to waste on boring things. You know that. But thanks to Ray, you don't have to waste precious weekends and holidays because of vague feelings of guilt or duty. With his Law of the Lifetime Remainder, you can calculate your losses and just say no.

Scared by the thought that you have only fifteen hundred weekends left? Wait till you hear Ray's other statistics. "If you're forty, you have only thirty more Thanksgivings. And thirty Christmases."

That should give you the perfect excuse to avoid your awful relatives. I can hear the liberating conversations in households across the nation: "You want me to spend Christmas at your mother's? I only have thirty left. I'm not wasting one on a woman who tells everyone you could have married better. I'd rather be with people who like me."

You aren't being selfish when you phrase it this way. You're making an appeal for family feeling.

As you get older these excuses will sound more poignant. At age fifty you can say, "How can you ask me to cook for the whole family again this year, when I only have twenty Thanksgivings left?"

Notice these reasons can be used for men and women. They are equally good for getting out of boring wedding or baby showers, Tupperware parties, and other female obligations.

Your remaining years will become truly golden once you

free yourself from dreary Sunday dinners and mind-numbing visits to the relatives. Your marriage will be burdened with fewer resentments and obligations. And when you turn down an unwanted invitation, you won't have to lie. You can refuse with the truth: "I'd like to come, but I just don't have the time."

The Law of the Lifetime Remainder can add many happy years to your marriage. You'll need every one. You're sure to encounter the kind of marital emergency that can take a few years off your life. One sign that your marriage will last for years is when you both pull together in the face of an emergency. And when Alexandra showed her face at our door, we faced real trouble.

Alexandra came to dinner early. Anyone knows that dinner at 8:00 means 8:15, at least. A party at 8:00 never gets going before 8:30. Anything earlier is cruel. At 8:00 P.M., your hosts are still running around, yelling at children and chucking things into closets.

I had no idea she would do this to me. Alexandra was a friend, who had helped me many times, which is why I invited her to dinner. She was also a white-bread WASP, who thought dinner in my solid German neighborhood was an exotic ethnic experience equal to a visit to India.

Alexandra refused to believe me when I said I was a lousy cook. I wanted to take her out for dinner. The more I said, "I don't cook," the more she decided I was just being modest. She refused to meet me at a restaurant. She was coming to my house for an exotic German meal. I knew from the sausage-and-sauerkraut dinners of my childhood that this was a contradiction in terms.

I finally found an old family recipe—an old Italian family. Raffaele, the guy who ran the Italian restaurant down the block, said he would cook dinner for us. He'd make veal marsala. All we'd have to do was throw it in the oven and throw out the boxes. Raffaele said he'd bring the dinner at a quarter to eight. He had everything, right down to the salad and crusty Italian bread.

At a quarter to eight, the house was in preguest chaos, but I was confident I'd have everything under control in half an hour. I was vacuuming the rug when I heard a knock on the back door. That was Raffaele with the food. Then the front doorbell rang. That was Alexandra, fifteen minutes early. Only, since she really shouldn't be at our house until 8:15, she was half an hour early. I was still in a pink bathrobe. Newspapers, clothes, shoes, dishes, and other debris still needed to be cleared away.

A lesser man would have slipped out the back with Raffaele. But Don stood by me. "What do you want me to do?" he asked. Whatever it was, it would have to be quick. Alexandra was leaning on the doorbell like a bill collector.

"Keep her occupied on the front porch," I said and ran for the back door.

Don kept Alexandra on the porch for ten minutes. It wasn't easy to stand there chatting and casually blocking the door when it was three below in January, but he managed. Meanwhile, I ran up the back steps with the dinner from Raffaele and stuffed it in the oven, except the salads. Then I grabbed everything that was lying around and shoved it in closets, under the bed, under the couch, and in the cabinets. As long as you didn't open any doors, the house looked pretty good.

It worked. Alexandra sailed in and sat down to dinner. "This veal marsala is delicious," she said. "Could you give me the recipe?"

"I couldn't," I simpered. "It's not mine to give. It belongs to the family."

"I understand," she said, humbly.

She couldn't possibly. I sure didn't understand what a German family was doing with a recipe for veal marsala.

After dinner, she admired our house. She even praised the spotless kitchen. "Now I know you're really a scrubby-clean German," she said. "After a meal like that, there's not a dirty dish in the kitchen." There were plenty of dirty carry-out boxes in the trash, but she didn't see those.

When Alexandra left at eleven P.M., Don and I breathed a sigh of relief. For weeks afterward we found shoes, mail, and small appliances in odd places. But I'll never figure out how the deed to the house got under the claw-foot bathtub.

My dinner with Alexandra could have been chaos. I was grateful that Don pitched in and helped handle the crisis.

And so I signed on for another year of monogamy.

It's not enough to help your partner when a crisis comes up. You have to know her so well, you can anticipate trouble and provide the solution before the problem happens. Don has mastered this marital art. For instance, he knew I would eventually be arrested for speeding and that I would not have enough money for bail—which is why, when we drove to Chicago, he always secretly carried enough cash to spring me from any speed trap.

I didn't know he did this. And I wouldn't have believed I needed him to bail me out. But, as he suspected, it happened. It was a rare warm day in late winter. I had a rare day off work, and rarest of all, I was driving a red Jaguar. Now I was tearing down Interstate 55. The car ripped along the gray highway like a razor through silver silk. In less than an hour we were at Litchfield, Illinois, fifty miles from St. Louis. We'd be in Chicago by supper time. The Jag was Don's dream car. He rarely let anyone else sit in his car, much less drive it. But he trusted me to take it to Chicago.

Maybe it's because I have an honest face. Maybe it's because we've been married so long.

Don popped in a new Buddy Holly tape. It was the drum solo from "Peggy Sue." I don't know if you've ever heard it, but that pounding drum sets the blood racing. I cranked up the volume. Then I cranked up the car. Then I saw the Illinois highway patrol car. But not before he saw me. He was on the other side of the divided highway. I thought that made me out of season. But he pulled a U-turn across two lanes of oncoming traffic, crossed the median strip, and pulled me over.

"I clocked you at eighty-nine," the officer said. "Your driver's license, ma'am."

I was calm. I reached in my wallet and handed him my credit card. He handed it back. It was over the limit, too.

The officer's name was Savage. But he didn't look it. He looked young. Even younger than doctors look these days. This means I am a taxpayer and semirespectable citizen. But I can't help it. I grew up in the sixties. Whenever I see anything with a badge and a uniform, I break out in a cold sweat and want to flush everything in my purse down the toilet.

The officer told me to follow him back to patrol headquarters. On the way, Don offered this advice: "Pretend he's a nine-hundred-pound gorilla. No matter what he says, tell him 'Yes, sir.'"

"Are you the newspaper columnist?" the officer said.

"Yes, sir." That's me. The fastest columnist in the Midwest.

"I don't meet many celebrities," he said. "I'm scared."

"I don't feel too good, either."

"You know I can't let you off," he said.

"I'm not asking for any favors," I said. I remembered that line from a forties prison movie. I thought it sounded cool.

"You'll have to post bail," the officer said. "It's seventy dollars cash."

I opened my wallet and everything fell out on the floor. Including three $1 bills. That was all the cash I had with me. Don posted bail from his secret stash. "I give good bond," he said.

"I'm going to fight it," I told him later.

"But you're guilty," said Don.

Guilty people get off all the time for crimes like murder and robbery. Remember the guy who killed the San Francisco mayor? He got off with voluntary manslaughter because he ate junk food—called it the Twinkie defense! I'd had a blameless record for twenty years. Then, suddenly, I got caught going an insane speed. It wasn't my fault. I was driven crazy by the Buddy Holly drum solo. I had the "drum defense."

My friends were unsympathetic. "You're just one of those jerks who passes me on the highway," said one.

The drum defense also failed to impress my attorney. He said we had a real hanging judge. The best I could hope for was parole. I would pay a fat fine and be released under the supervision of the court for three months.

The red brick courthouse was in nearby Hillsboro, Illinois. It had a neon sign that said, THE WORLD NEEDS GOD. "Oh, Lord," said the lawyer, when he saw the sign. I think he read it as ALL HOPE ABANDON, YE WHO ENTER HERE.

The lawyer tried. He told the judge this ticket would put one whopping zit on my unblemished record. He said it would raise my insurance. The judge said he could make no exceptions. Then the lawyer said the same thing all over again. So did the judge.

Then I pleaded guilty.

"I'm sorry," the lawyer said.

"Me, too. If I'd been arrested for murder, you might have had something to work with."

Don's seventy-dollar bailout on an Illinois interstate bought me another year of monogamy. I figured the man knew me better than I knew myself.

If Don's high-speed bailout surprised me, so did his care when I broke my hip. I knew we'd promised to stand by one another in sickness and in health. But I made that promise at twenty-one. I didn't ever really expect to be sick. At age forty, I fell in an ice storm and wound up with a total hip replacement.

I was helpless and I hated it. But then, I hated everything when I was sick, especially being waited on. I was not a patient patient. I hated sleeping flat on my back in a rented hospital bed in our bedroom. I hated that Don had to bring up dinners made for me by friends and relatives. I hated hobbling down the hall to the bathroom with a walker, like an old woman.

But I hated most that I couldn't even bend over and flush the toilet. Don had to do that, too. I was humiliated.

He did everything well except trying to get me to laugh. Nothing seemed funny. I began to think I'd rather be single, so I wouldn't have to bother the person I loved with these wretched chores. Don finally got me laughing at the least likely location—the hospital. I went back for a routine checkup. I screwed up the courage to ask my dour orthopedic surgeon about sex, since the hip plays a fairly large part in that activity. The surgeon looked like I'd just asked him for Madonna's home phone number. He was mystified by my request. "I don't know what to tell you," he said. "None of my patients have ever asked that before. My hip patients are usually very old, and they don't have sex lives."

The physical therapist was more helpful. She gave me a

handmade hospital-issue booklet, published on the copier machine, called something like *Sex for Cripples*. It explained that for several months, missionary and anything else familiar was out. Instead, we'd have to use some other positions to ease the strain on my healing hip. The booklet had some illustrations. I looked at them with dismay. They seemed uncomfortable and complicated. I wasn't sure I could put my left leg behind my right ear. I couldn't even figure out knitting instructions.

Don studied the pictures with curiosity. Most curious of all, the copulating couples were all modestly dressed in fifties-style bathing suits.

"Do we have to wear the bathing suits?" he said.

For the first time in weeks, I started laughing. His funny remark banished my doubts. I could commit monogamy for one more year.

I didn't think there was anything funny when Don was rushed to the hospital with an asthma attack. But while the doctors worked on him, the orange-vested EMT brought me a pile of papers to sign. One paper described Don as a "chronic SOB."

"He's not chronic," I said. "Only occasional."

"SOB stands for shortness of breath," said the EMT.

I'm convinced Don stayed with me year after year because, although I had my faults, I was never boring. Even when we had a slug fest, it was innovative. It started in the kitchen, where so many do.

"Wanna buy some beer for the slugs?" I asked Don.

"That's no way to talk about my friends," he said.

"I'm not. I'm talking about those squishy snaillike garden pests. They're chewing on my plants in the backyard. The experts say the best way to get rid of night-crawling slugs is to drown them in beer."

"At least they die happy," Don said.

Normally, I hate yardwork. It's hard, sweaty, and dull. But getting slugs soused every night seemed a more interesting chore than cutting the grass. Here were the directions on how to slug a slug, from a wire-service story: "Sink shallow tin, especially clean pet food cans, flush with the soil level and pour in beer until the cans are half full," the garden expert advised. "Slugs are attracted to the scent, fall in, and drown."

Slugs aren't the only pests who drown themselves in beer. I knew a couple of guys who tried it, too. I wondered if drunken slugs sang "Proud Mary." Putting out beer beat another slug killing method. "Table salt poured on their backs will destroy them," the garden expert said.

I refused to sit in the backyard with a salt shaker, waiting for a slug to crawl by. Besides, beer is environmentally sound. It is a natural blend of barley, malt, hops, and yeast. There are no harmful ingredients to poison the earth. Sorry I can't say the same for beer's effect on the human liver.

Beer is cheap, too. Don and I checked out the prices in the supermarket cooler. A quart of malt liquor was less than two bucks, but I was afraid even slugs wouldn't touch that stuff. "What do you think slugs drink?" I asked.

"I like Scotch myself," Don said.

There was no Slug Lite, so we decided to give them a Rocky Mountain high. We settled on a quart of Coors. That night, I went out to the backyard with my beer and a shallow dish to start the slug fest. The next morning, I wasn't expecting much. It had been raining hard. But the dish was filled with about fifty dead slugs, floating on their watery beer. They were small and nasty looking, an ugly greenish brown. Some were only the size of fingernail parings. A few fat ones were an inch long. One had a tattoo and a tiny

CAT hat. There's something satisfying about throwing out a bunch of dead drunks. I knew they wouldn't be wandering around burping and scratching and complaining that their heads hurt. I probably did them a favor. There's nothing worse than crawling around with a hangover.

The next night, I poured the slugs more beer. I was turning into a serial slug killer, and it felt good. The next morning, I checked the dish again. This time there were a dozen slugged slugs. Served them right.

The third night, I was heading out to the backyard with my cold quart when Don stopped me. "Where are you going with the beer?" he said.

"It's for the slugs."

"Any left over for me?" he asked.

"Sure," I said. "Name your poison." That was one more advantage to beer. How many other pesticides can you drink?

We toasted another year of monogamy. We'd both need that drink. I didn't know it yet, but the next year, we'd be moving to Washington, D.C., the city that didn't work, living in an apartment where nothing worked except the occupants.

If I ever walked out of the marriage, this would be the year. And yet, I hung in there. I knew things would get better.

The next year, I was fired.

Once I got over the shock, I was surprised to discover I liked working at home with Don. I used to hear my German aunts complain when their husbands retired, "I married him for better or worse, but not for lunch."

Now we were both home for breakfast, lunch, and dinner. We held editorial conferences on the second-floor landing, "What do you think of this paragraph?" I'd say, and he'd read it and pass judgement. We'd give ourselves the afternoon off (when you're self-employed, you have good bosses) and go for a walk.

Now that we both worked at home, we no longer wasted time talking about office politics, stupid memos, or stupid bosses. And we really liked that.

The year that I thought would be the worst turned out to be the best.

After twenty-five years, we've learned that monogamy is not for sissies.

We don't have a traditional marriage, the way my family hoped: Don doesn't go off to work with his briefcase, and I don't stay home with the 2.5 children and have a pot roast on the table when he comes home.

We don't have a marriage till death do us part.

What we have is marriage American style—one year at a time.

It lasts longer that way.